managing money

Skills in Action

managing money
money matters for managers

Roy H Hill OBE
FMCA, MCIM, FCMC, FCIPD

CIM Publishing

CIM Publishing

The Chartered Institute of Marketing
Moor Hall
Cookham
Berkshire
SL6 9QH

www.cim.co.uk

First published 2002
© CIM Publishing 2002

All rights reserved. No part of this publication may be reproduced in any material form (including photocopying or storing in any medium by electronic means and whether or not transiently or inadvertently to some other use of this publication) without the prior written permission of the copyright holder, except in provisions of the Copyright, Designs and Patents Act 1988 or under the terms of a licence issued by the Copyright Licensing Agency Ltd., 90 Tottenham Court Road, London, England, W1P 9HE.

Applications for the copyright holder's written permission to reproduce any part of this publication should be addressed to the publishers.
This book may not be lent, resold, hired out or otherwise disposed of in any form of binding or cover other than that in which it is published.

British Library Cataloguing in Publication Data
A CIP catalogue record for this book can be obtained from the British Library.

ISBN 0 902130 62 5

The publishers believe that the contents of this book contribute to debate and offer practical advice. No responsibility will be taken by the publishers for any damage or loss arising from following or interpreting the advice given in this publication.

It is the publisher's policy to use paper manufactured from sustainable forests.

Typesetting by Columns Design Ltd., Reading, Berkshire.
Printed and bound by The Cromwell Press, Trowbridge, Wiltshire.
Cover design by ABA Associates, Ascot, Berkshire.

about the author

Roy H Hill is a Chartered Management Accountant and Chartered Marketer, specialising in interpreting finance for non-financial managers. His executive experience includes senior management positions in the clothing, furniture and chemical industries. He has also been a senior partner with an international management consultancy firm, covering a variety of industries and assignments.

Roy is the Founder President of the Institute of Business Advisers, a qualified assessor under the NCVQ schemes, and holds public practice certificates from CIMA, ICSA and IMC.

He has led courses on 'Marketing in focus' and 'Finance for Non-Financial Executives' and run senior management programmes for major organisations both in the UK and internationally.

In 1991 he was appointed an OBE for his advisory services to small firms through schemes set up by government departments.

dedication

To Dorice, my wife, for her encouragement and feedback.

general acknowledgement

Thousands of people influenced, instructed and helped me to form my opinions and attitudes – some unwittingly and many personally unknown to me.

There is one group of people, however, originally led by George Sanders and Fred Pritchett, now banded together in the Lyndall Urwick Society, to whom I would like to record my sincere thanks for their part in my management education.

contents

Preface ix

PART A	**The Business as a Whole**	**1**
Session 1	Why is the money needed?	3
Session 2	Where does it come from?	13
Session 3	Have we done well? Will we survive?	25
PART B	**The Business from Inside**	**41**
Session 4	Working Capital	43
Session 5	Planning for Profit	57
Session 6	Budgeting and Control	73
Session 7	The Marginal Approach – Costs for Decision Making	87
Session 8	Investment Appraisal	99
Session 9	Management Accounting	111
APPENDICES		**123**
Appendix 1	Forms of Business Ownership	125
Appendix 2	Accounting Concepts	129
Appendix 3	Glossary of Accounting Terms	131
Appendix 4	An Introduction to Double Entry Bookkeeping	139
Index		143

preface

Managing Money probably ranks as one of the most neglected areas of a typical manager's education. Responsibility for the management of resources, whether human, physical or intellectual (and frequently it is all three!), inevitably brings a financial responsibility with it. This accountability can become a perpetual and all-consuming problem if we are not equipped to deal with it but, even worse, it means we cannot make a full contribution to business success if we are not fully aware of the financial consequences of our decisions and recommendations.

This book seeks to provide an introduction to the financial aspects of management in business. The principles are straightforward, logical and have arisen from the practical needs of business people over the centuries.

Which brings us to the question – what do we mean by business? A definition that I like comes from my colleagues Fred Pritchett and Ed Lambert, at Urwick Orr and Partners Limited. They convinced me that 'Business is any organised social and economic activity'. For example, if you throw a party it is certainly social, it may even be organised but it is unlikely to be economic! Organise a party, charge enough for tickets to attend and then it becomes economic too: now it is business!

The examples given in this book are primarily based on business ownership in the form of a private Limited Liability Company, unless otherwise stated.

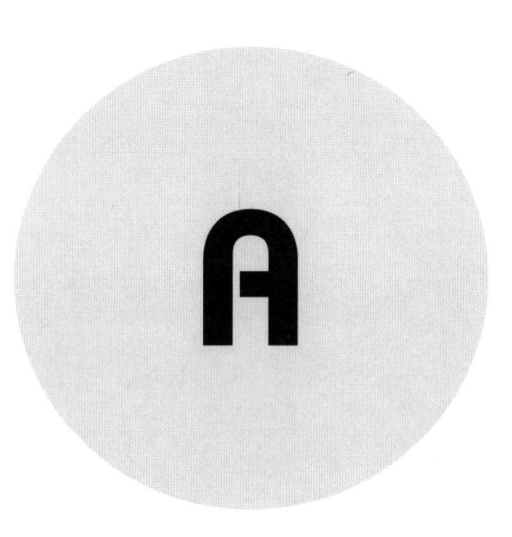

part

A

session

1

why is the money needed?

Our first reaction to the emotive word **MONEY** is probably to think of great heaps of notes and coins – money in its spendable form, **CASH**. But we are also aware that we can use 'money' to represent **VALUES**. Indeed, houses are valued in money terms, frequently for far more than was paid for them!

Taking these two points together we can say that **MONEY** provides:

- A medium of exchange (goods and services in exchange for cash).
- A measure of value (we can compare unlike things on the common basis of money values).

In business both of these aspects are important. We don't always pay immediate cash for everything we own – most people buy a house with a mortgage for example. In this book 'money' is generally treated as an equivalent word for 'cash', but we also need a word that embraces money values, commitments and sources as well. The most appropriate word is **FINANCE**. House buying is usually financed by some cash plus a mortgage. Businesses need finance in the same way. Rarely can everything be done on a cash basis, therefore financial instruments such as loans, mortgages, bills of exchange, hire purchase and leases to name but a few, have been developed to facilitate the smooth operation of a business.

As we shall see, money, in the form of cash, is necessary for day-to-day survival, but finance is essential for long-term survival and growth.

why businesses need finance

If we were starting a business we would need to equip ourselves with a range of essential resources. The resources would have to be available ahead of satisfying our customers and before the costs of those resources can be recovered by our selling prices. The finance required would also be affected by the anticipated levels of activity. Our business activity can be seen as a series of cycles, each of which ties up finance. These cycles include:

group 1 – the setting up and development cycle

- **Land and premises** – one or more bases from which to operate.
- **Machinery and equipment** – operational machines and equipment, vehicles etc. (needed for the products, marketing, research, maintenance, administration and other activities).

The formation of the business itself will usually incur professional and fiscal charges, but these should not be significant in the long run. Developments will occur in varying degrees, both continuously and at intervals during the life of the business, to extend or change its activities. These changes may also involve investment expenditure.

group 2 – up and running

- **The First Storage Cycle**
- **Materials** – for use in the product, for packaging, promotions, administration, research or maintenance.
- **The Operating Cycle**
  Work in Progress – in anticipation of orders, or to satisfy orders received. The operating cycle is concerned with providing the saleable work of the business, i.e. goods or services (see note opposite).
- **The Second Storage Cycle**
  Finished Work – unless the goods or services pass immediately to the purchaser by delivery, implementation or agreement (see note opposite).

WHY IS THE MONEY NEEDED?

- **The Distribution Cycle**
  Transfer to the customer from storage or operations may involve a physical delivery by road, rail, sea, air or transmission line; it may be combined with other deliveries or be a special shipment.
- **The Credit Cycle**
  Debtors – in business-to-business transactions the payment is unlikely to be made immediately on delivery or performance. A period of credit is typically allowed, determined by trade practice or negotiation. We are, therefore, still financing the products that they have bought. The degree of success in securing payment within terms has a significant effect on the credit cycle.
- **Cash** – held to deal with contingencies, cope with seasonal demands and to enable day-to-day business to proceed.

Note: the values of work in progress and finished work would include the value added by people, services and other costs directly relevant to the products at the stage reached.

It is important that active, effective, management controls are maintained for each of these cycles. Management techniques are available to assist, but it is effective managers who implement them for results.

The total finance employed in our business has to be sufficient to sustain all the cycles described above. Delays in completing any of the cycles are forms of under-utilisation of resources, which leads to reduced profits.

> **management techniques** are available to assist, but it is **effective managers** who implement them for **results**

The total finance we employ is equal to the **TOTAL ASSETS** owned by our business.

comment

The first group above consists, typically, of relatively high-value and long-life items, whereas the second group will be in a continuing state of flux. Our products may take the form of goods, services or a combination of the two. Our customers may be other businesses or retail consumers. Finance is needed to provide and support all these resources. In accounting terms these resources are the **ASSETS** of our business.

This can all be summed up as 'Businesses need finance to meet the necessary outgoings before their customers pay them'. The finance is the investment and therefore a return on the investment will be expected.

> businesses need **finance** to meet the necessary **outgoings** before their customers **pay** them

so how much do we need?

There are many influences on the amount of finance needed, for example:

- **Speed of Sale** – how quickly do we expect sales to occur? A baker expects to make steady sales daily, but a jeweller cannot make such an assumption! A civil engineering company may constantly be looking for large contracts, but they will probably be obtained only at irregular intervals. Finance needs tend to be greater when the speed of sale is irregular and the operational cycle lengthy.
- **Scale of Operation** – is our output based on mass production or are we small scale? Are our products within a limited range, or is every project different? Are our products tangible goods and/or in the form of services? The need for finance tends to be greater where there are high-cost products and a variable demand.
- **Seasonality** – where sales are concentrated into limited times of the year expenditure and income flows may be significantly unsynchronised. This will mean that we will require bridging finance during the lower sales periods.
- **Length of Chain** – if our business operates as a group of discrete activities it may be organised as if each member of the group is making sales to another member, so that a product may go through several buy/sell transactions (links in the chain) before a real sale to a third party takes place. It is only after the final link, the external sale, that genuine new money enters our business. The previous transactions were all on paper. It is the overall operational cycle for our group that has to be financed. The greater the number of links the greater may be the need for finance.

recovering the finance

The selling prices we adopt have to be sufficient to cover our total resources, including the operating elements that have gone into the product, either directly or indirectly. The premises, plant and equipment (the **tangible fixed assets**) may have a relatively long life but, over that life, their cost has also to be 'recovered'. This is done by estimating the **economic** life of these assets and relating the cost of each asset to its economic life (remember that the physical life may prove to be even longer, but later developments may make any continued use uneconomic). The rate of technological and other relevant changes is not constant, and estimates of economic life have to be reviewed from time to time, particularly in times of significant inflation when replacement costs can be much higher.

The forecasting of economic life usually follows the **'PESTLE'** sequence to consider future changes and their impact:

- **Political** – are new statutory requirements likely to have an impact?
- **Economic** – are booms and depressions expected to have an impact on demand?
- **Social** – are market and socio-economic changes likely to change demand?
- **Technological** – are there expectations of change, or alternative methods which could render our equipment obsolete?
- **Legal** – are new regulations anticipated which could affect our projects?
- **Environmental** – are any new attitudes emerging which could affect the projects?

It can be useful to develop project checklists if similar projects recur.

depreciation

The name given to the expense introduced into our operating costs to represent the consumption of our tangible fixed assets is **depreciation**. A similar amount is deducted from the value of the asset(s) concerned. There are two methods in general use to assess the depreciation amounts, but each depends on the estimate of the economic life of the asset concerned. For example:

MANAGING MONEY

Equipment costing £9,000 has been purchased. The project team has done a PESTLE forecast to estimate its economic life. They have decided that it will be five years.

The depreciation amount will, therefore, be £9,000, to be recovered over 5 years. The most popular method of calculating annual depreciation is probably **straight line.** For this, the value to be depreciated (£9,000), is divided by the economic life (5 yr). This means that £1,800 per annum (£150 per month) will be charged as depreciation.

The other depreciation method is called **reducing balance** – although not as popular as the straight line method it is still used by some businesses (and by the Inland Revenue in their calculations of capital allowances for business tax purposes).

This method applies an agreed percentage rate to reduce the asset value each year – the amount of the reduction is charged as depreciation in that year. Unlike the straight line method, it is calculated on the ever reducing value, not the original value. The percentage used may be calculated exactly, or rounded figures applied which approximate to the economic life assessed. In practice it is likely that a nice round figure of 50% would be used for a 5-year life, with any over- or under-charge adjusted in the final year.

A comparison of the two methods is given in the table below. You can see that when the reducing balance method is used, the amount of depreciation is substantially more than twice as much in year 1 compared to the straight line approach, but in later years the position is reversed.

DEPRECIATION METHODS Years	Yr 1	Yr 2	Yr 3	Yr 4	Yr 5	TOTAL
Straight Line	1,800	1,800	1,800	1,800	1,800	9,000
Reducing Balance – 50%	4,500	2,250	1,125	563	281	8,719
Reducing Balance – 50% adjusted	4,500	2,250	1,125	563	562	9,000

Fig 1.1

WHY IS THE MONEY NEEDED?

DEPRECIATION METHODS

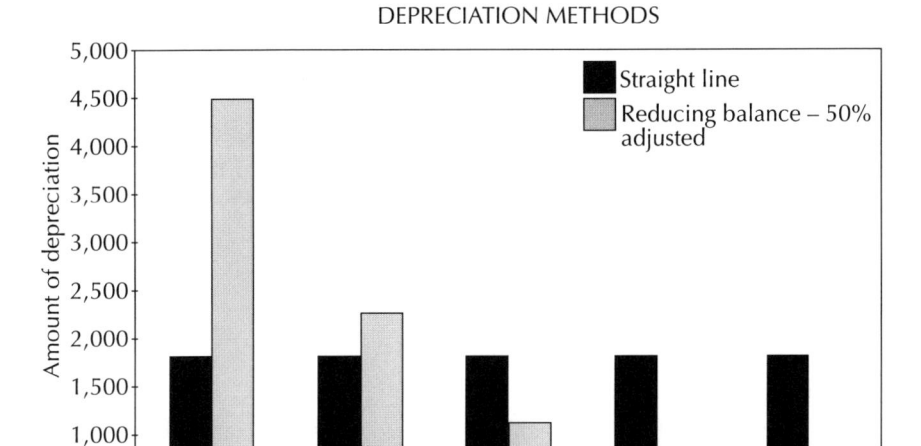

Fig 1.2

Other methods may be used; some are based on operating hours per period rather than the calendar itself, some are unit output based per period (how many miles did the vehicle run, or how many photocopies were made?).

An interesting variation on the reducing balance method described above is called 'sum of the digits'. It is claimed to be widely used in Asia and works like this:

> Add up the year numbers – for a 5-year life this means 1+2+3+4+5 equals 15. Divide the investment by this number – in our case £9,000 would be divided by 15, to give £600.
>
> | | | | | | |
> |---|---|---|---|---|---|
> | Then in | Year 1 | charge | 5 × £600 | = | £3,000 |
> | | Year 2 | | 4 × £600 | = | £2,400 |
> | | Year 3 | | 3 × £600 | = | £1,800 |
> | | Year 4 | | 2 × £600 | = | £1,200 |
> | | Year 5 | | 1 × £600 | = | £ 600 |
> | A total depreciation charge over 5 years of | | | | | £9,000 |

comment

Depreciation represents the usage of the tangible fixed assets of the business in the course of its operations. There is no one method that can be claimed as correct. Because of the relative simplicity of the straight line method it appears to be the most used at present.

revaluation

Some tangible assets, such as property in good areas, are seen to be appreciating rather than depreciating. Where the appreciation is regarded as significant and not temporary, a decision may be made to have a revaluation carried out by appropriate experts.

Depreciation would then continue to be charged but at the modified rates required by the enhanced value. The remaining economic life of the asset may also be reviewed at the same time, further modifying the depreciation charge if necessary.

The increase in value of the asset represents an **unrealised** profit for the shareholders of the business. It did not arise from normal trading and so it appears as an **Asset Revaluation Reserve** with the other shareholder funds, as we shall see later.

session

2

where does it come from?

There are three major sources of finance:

1. The Shareholders (or Proprietors)
2. The Lenders:
   - Long term (more than one year)
   - Short term (within one year)
3. Other Creditors:
   - Suppliers
   - Employees – paid in arrears, very short term!
   - Fiscal (VAT, Corporation Tax, Employer/employee deductions…)

Shareholders expect to be rewarded by regular, ever increasing, dividends, plus an accompanying increase in the underlying value of their shares from the retention of profits. It is rare for all the profits to be paid out as dividends. The **Retained Profits** accumulate within the **Shareholder Funds** and form the **Revenue Reserves** of the company.

The amount of dividend is determined by the directors. Dividends can only be paid if there is money available, but a typical level is around one third of the profits, two thirds being retained. The dividend is expressed as 'per share'.

Shareholders accept that there is no guarantee of profits being generated (or increasing) each year, and they realise that they will bear the brunt of any failure to make profits. Firstly dividends would be reduced, as would the reserves if losses are sustained, and finally the underlying share values themselves would be reduced or eliminated by the losses.

If a company is listed on the Stock Exchange, the **Market Price**, also expressed per share, will rise or fall according to the opinions of buyers and sellers, based upon their interpretation of the company's position and attitudes to the industry in which it operates. Unlisted companies are less concerned with Stock Exchange views, but may find difficulty raising additional finance if their profit record is unsatisfactory in the eyes, or pockets, of potential investors!

Lenders are a mixture of financial institutions, other companies and individuals.

Long-term loans may take the form of specific amounts, for specific periods, at fixed rates of interest; they may be **Convertible Bonds** (that is, there may be an option to convert the loan into ordinary shares by a pre-arranged formula). Other long-term forms may be **Finance Leases** in connection with **Tangible Assets** (such as property or industrial vehicles). Debentures are formal loans, given under the Company Seal, and usually include a formal charge on one or more assets of the company as security.

Short-term lending (potentially repayable within one year) includes overdrafts, specific term loans, bills of exchange and long-term debt in its final year.

What lenders have in common is that they require both interest payments and loan repayments (whether in periodic instalments or in total) to be made in accordance with the conditions of the loans, irrespective of whether the business is profitable or not.

Other creditors are the suppliers of goods and services ('**Trade Creditors**'), who are waiting to be paid. We may also have 'fiscal' creditors – monies due to government departments for Corporation Tax, Value Added Tax (VAT), employees' Pay As You Earn (PAYE) deductions from their wages but not yet handed over, National Insurance (NI) contributions, also deducted from wages together with the employer's contributions. All of these have to be paid within credit limits. There may also be pension contributions awaiting transfer to the provider.

Pre-payment is when we have received payment in advance from our customers for goods or services not yet delivered or performed. These too would normally be shown within the **Current Liabilities** as creditors, until we have carried out our commitments. Travel and financial services are examples of businesses that have to be particularly careful to identify such items, and are often required to set up separate bank accounts to hold the money.

The credit provided by pre-payment is very useful, as we do not have to make interest payments to the providers. It is a very economic form of finance! It is worth remembering though that we provide a similar benefit to our customers when we give them credit.

the sources and applications of finance

Having assessed our needs for finance (the **Fixed** and **Current Assets**) and identified the sources of finance (the shareholder funds, the lenders and the other creditors) we have arrived at the five main sections of the **Balance Sheet**.

The prime purpose of a balance sheet is to show the position of a business at a particular time, usually as at midnight (accountants always work late!) on the final day of an accounting period. It shows what the business owns in assets, and how these assets are financed by the sources of finance – shareholders, lenders and other creditors. The following table summarises this essential information.

comment

> the **prime** purpose of a **balance sheet** is to show the **position of a business** at a particular time

The five sections of the UK balance sheet are required to appear in the order shown overleaf in the columnar form, widely used today. It is a requirement that the **Current Liabilities** should be deducted from the **Current Assets** and thus show the **Net Current Assets**. There is therefore no total assets figure given within the balance sheet, nor any total sources in this format.

Intangible assets are a comparatively recent focus of interest: they include goodwill, patents, purchased know-how, trademarks and brand values. The accounting concept of prudence encouraged playing down the intangible values, especially as they are somewhat subjective. However, recently it has became clear that many take-over bids are based on an asset value that includes intangibles, particularly brand values. Undervaluing intangibles encourages unwelcome attention.

The long-term investments included in the fixed asset total represent investment **by** the company. These investments may be held for several reasons: ownership of subsidiaries; to form a link with customers or

The Balance Sheet – the five main sections

Fixed Assets	Intangible
	Tangible
	Investments – long term
Current Assets	Stocks (Inventories)
	Debtors (Accounts Receivable)
	Investments – short term
	Cash/Bank
Current Liabilities	Trade Creditors (Accounts Payable)
(Creditors due within one year)	Other Creditors – e.g. Corporation Tax
	Overdraft/Short-term loans
Creditors due after more than one year & Provisions	Long-term loans
	Provision for future tax
Shareholders' Funds	Preference Shares
	Net Worth: Ordinary Shares,
	Capital Reserves
	e.g. Share Premium,
	Asset Revaluation,
	Revenue Reserves
	(from Operating
	Profits retained)

Note: What we own: Fixed Assets
+ Current Assets

equals

What we owe: Current Liabilities
+ Creditors due after more than one year
+ Shareholders' Funds

Fig 2.1

suppliers; to provide a toe-hold for a future bid, or perhaps to ensure that finance will be available to replace a major asset at the end of its useful life. In mining, for example, it was appreciated that after several years the target ore would run out and a new mine shaft would have to be sunk elsewhere to continue the business – hence the name 'sinking fund' given to this type of investment. Shipping companies may similarly build up funds to replace their major vessels but would probably avoid using the same term!

Preference Shares, included in shareholders' funds, typically have a fixed rate of dividend, and are 'preferentially' entitled to this payment before ordinary shareholders. Similarly, they have preferential rights over the ordinary shareholders to repayment of their investment in the event of the company being wound up. It is usual these days for preference shares to be 'convertible'. This means that the holders have a pre-agreed rate of conversion of their preference shares into ordinary shares at agreed times. Other types of preference share include:

- **Cumulative**. This means that if the company is unable to pay their dividend in any year, the arrears of dividend will become a preferential claim when the company moves back into profit and can pay dividends once more.
- **Redeemable**. This offers the opportunity of repayment to the holder according to the terms of issue.
- **Participating**. Here the preference shareholders may receive in addition to the fixed dividend, and according to the terms of issue, a second element linked to overall company performance.

Capital Reserves arise when:

(a) **Tangible Assets** are increased on re-valuation. The benefit of the increase is attributable to the ordinary shareholders, but as it has not arisen from operating profits it cannot therefore be part of revenue reserves. Instead it becomes a **Capital Reserve**, the 'Asset Revaluation Reserve'.

(b) If a company decides to raise more finance from shareholders it offers additional shares as a **Rights Issue** to existing shareholders, in proportion to their existing holding. The price of the new shares cannot be below their face value, but if the company has done well, they may be able to adopt a price above it. Nominal value shares of £1 might be offered, say, at £2.50. The £1.50 difference is the **Share Premium**. The £1 equivalent to the nominal value goes to increase the **Ordinary Shares Issued** total and the £1.50 becomes part of the **Capital Reserve**, 'Share Premium Account'.

For example, say our company needs £500 to embark upon a wonderful new project. We have been advised to raise the money by a rights issue, on the basis of offering 2 new ordinary shares, with a face value of £1 each, at £2.50 each to all of the shareholders, in addition to the £1 share they each currently hold.

Before: 100 ordinary £1 shares in issue.   **Total value: £100**

After the issue of 200 additional ordinary £1 shares at £2.50 each

300 ordinary £1 shares in issue   £300
Share Premium Account (200 × £1.50)   £300
Total value: £600

The shareholders' funds have risen by £500 from what they were before, the amount needed for the new project. The cash proceeds from the issuing of these additional 200 shares would appear in the current assets section of the balance sheet as an increase in the cash at bank of £500. The project can then go ahead.

The **Issue Price** is normally based on the recommendation of the company's financial advisers, who may back their judgment by agreeing to take up any shares not bought by the shareholders entitled to them. This is called **Underwriting**, and it ensures that the company will get the finance it needs. The need may be to reduce dependence on borrowed money (by repaying loans from the issue receipts, as BT have recently done) or it may be to finance a major project.

The sources of finance should be matched to the needs. Long-term finance should be raised/used for long-term assets (don't buy your house with a six-week loan!). In practice, a prudent approach should ensure that there is always some long-term finance available, beyond the needs of the long-term assets, which will help finance some of the current assets, so that the business is not over-dependent on short-term finance.

the circulation of finance in a business

The circulating diagram opposite helps to illustrate how finance moves around a business in a continuous state of change. We start with a **Reservoir** (hydraulic terms seem to have an affinity with accounting!) of liquid, i.e. spendable assets. We obtain credit wherever we benefit from it and provide ourselves with both **Fixed Assets** and **Current Assets**. **Materials**, as part of our current assets, typically start in a **Stock** situation, before moving into **Operations** and having value added to them by sub-contractors, our own staff and bought-in services. A proportion of the fixed asset costs are also added in the form of **Depreciation**. The impact of the **Intangibles** may be to either enhance the perceived value in the

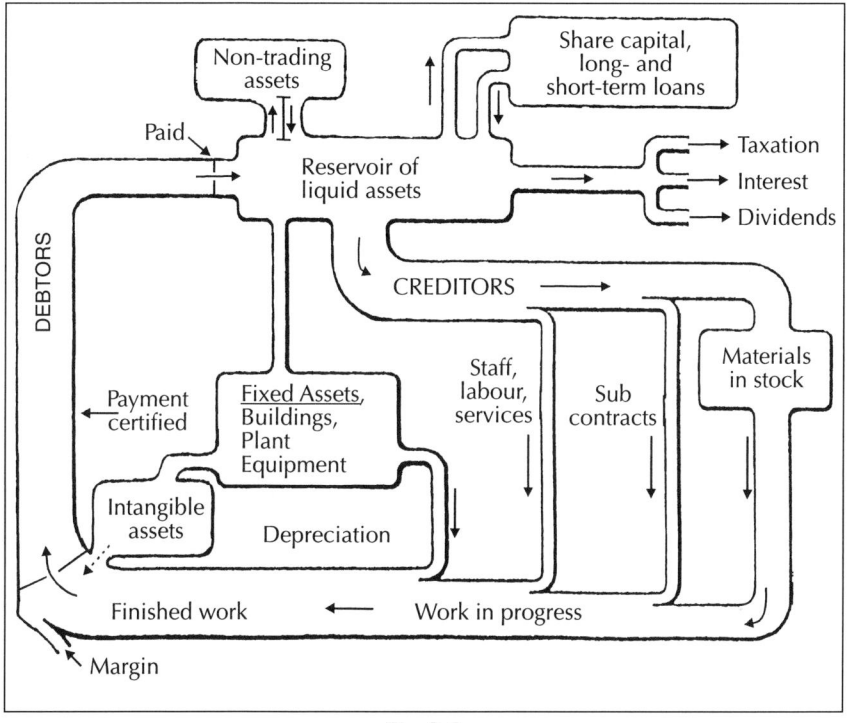

Fig 2.2

eyes of the purchasers, via a brand name perhaps, or to reduce the costs of operations by purchased know-how. In either case the effect is to increase the profit margin in our selling prices.

Once sold, we have **Debtors** who in due course pay us, and their money flows into the reservoir, replacing our expenditure over time, and providing a **Surplus** if we are successful. Part of this surplus will move out of the system because of **Taxation**, **Interest Payments** on loans and **Dividends** to our shareholders. We may use some of the surplus, on occasion, by making **Investments** of our own. We may also be raising finance by **Rights Issues** or **Loans**, and parting with money from the reservoir to repay earlier loans by instalment or in total.

An investment in **Non-Trading Assets** may arise from time to time. For example, we may own an office block that is larger than our immediate needs. It could be both sensible and economic to let part of it on short-term leases. There will be some expenditure for maintenance on the area let, and some income from the rents. We have, therefore, a discrete mini-system within our primary activities, but quite separate from our on-going business operations. If we are successful we can hopefully expand within our own building!

Our prime objective is to maintain, or preferably, increase the speed of circulation, so that we pass the point of sale more frequently and so increase both **Sales Revenue** and **Operating Profits**.

the growth of a business over time

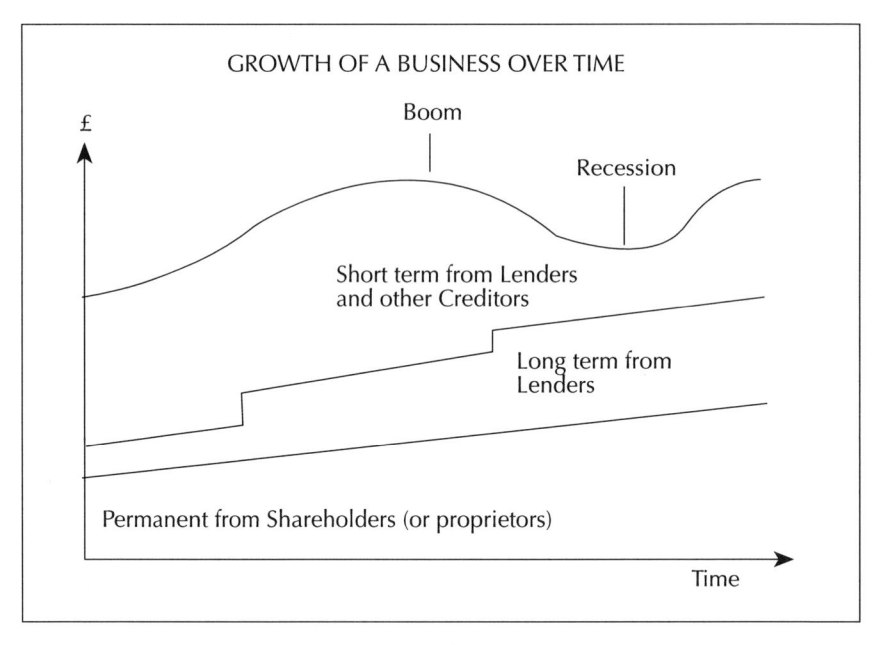

Fig 2.3

The diagram 'Growth of a Business Over Time', shows how the major sources of finance may develop. The permanent finance from the shareholders is rising because of the **Retained Profits** added to the **Revenue Reserve** each year. The increase would rarely be as smooth as here, but the trend should show an increase over the years. A rights issue would create a jump in the figures before resuming a new regular trend. However, the trend is likely to be at a slightly greater angle if the new finance produces additional profits.

Lenders relate the amount they are willing to lend to the amount of shareholder finance in the business. They like to see a good amount of

Equity (Risk) finance providing a cushion beneath their loans, as it makes them more secure. Long-term finance is usually negotiated in relatively large amounts – hence the steps shown in the long-term finance line.

Short-term finance can come from loans of a fixed amount for a limited period, or from the more flexible overdraft. It can also come from the suppliers of goods and services on conventional credit terms. As the diagram shows, this variable finance will rise in boom times and fall in recession. In boom times we have more short-term finance needs – to support the increased debtors (we are selling more), increased stocks (materials, work in progress and finished work) and we are probably investing in increasing our resources. But in recession our original debtors will pay their debts but may not order more, our operating stocks will fall because of reduced demand, and we are less likely to be increasing our resources. Short-term finance is largely elastic and so the increase and decrease in needs can be accommodated.

session

3

have we done well? will we survive?

comment

This session can be hard going for those of us who hate numbers and those of us who do not yet feel familiar with overall business objectives and the financial side of management.

It may be sensible therefore, to skim through this session on first reading, sufficient to gain a general idea of the contents, and then return later after reading the other sessions.

accounting ratios

The purpose of ratios is to provide measures of:

(a) **Profitability** – from the investors and managers point of view.
(b) **Financial security** – we need a sensible mixture of shareholder and borrowed finance, of long-term and short-term finance.
(c) **Solvency** – the ability to pay debts as they fall due.

There is no limit to the number of ratios which businesses or business analysts can use. Some may be peculiar to an industry (for example, sales per square metre in retail stores can be of great interest to the managers concerned), but those shown here are the most commonly used, and have been approved by the Ratio Relations Board. They cover aspects of profitability (Ratio Group 1), stability (Ratio Group 2) and solvency (Ratio Group 3). Many of these ratios are used in benchmarking.

a specimen company limited

The accounts of 'A Specimen Company Limited' are shown to form a basis from which we can establish some ideas about profitability, liquidity and financial security.

Normally ratios are based upon three years figures, so as to ascertain trends. Figures for two years are given in each Annual Report, so if you have two years' reports you will have the data for three years.

Abbreviations used

The following abbreviations are used in the Profit and Loss Account (Fig 3.1) and Balance Sheet (Fig 3.2). They are also used in the ratio calculations that follow them.

OpP   Operating Profit
PBT   Profit before tax
PAT   Profit after tax
FA   Fixed Assets
CA   Current Assets
CL   Current Liabilities (Creditors due within one year)
CA-CL   Net Current Assets. Generally Current Assets (CA) will exceed Current Liabilities (CL), though this is not always the case!
(TA-CL) = LTF   Total Assets (FA+CA) less Current Liabilities (CL) equals the Long-Term Finance of the business.
NW   Net Worth. The finance attributable to the Ordinary Shareholders.

When we deduct all third party finance (long-term lenders and other long- and short-term creditors) from the total assets of the business, we are left with the **Net Worth** of the business, which is the amount financed by the ordinary shareholders' investment. This consists of their shares, capital reserves (if any) and the accumulated retained profits transferred from the profit and loss account over the years – the revenue reserves.

HAVE WE DONE WELL?

A SPECIMEN COMPANY LIMITED

Profit and Loss Account: year ending 31 December 200X

	£000	Abbreviation
Sales	530	
Less Cost of Sales	390	
Gross Profit	140	
Less Distribution/Administrative Costs	40	
Operating Profit	100	OpP
Dividends/Interest received	–	
Interest Paid	(10)	
Profit Before Tax	90	PBT
Tax, say	30	
Profit After Tax	60	PAT
Dividends proposed	20	
Retained this year	40	To Balance Sheet, Net Worth (NW).

Fig 3.1

comment

The ratios included in this session are all derived from figures shown in the Profit and Loss Account and the Balance Sheet.

A level of Profit before the Operating Profit is, however, sometimes adopted. It is described as EBITDA (Earnings Before Interest, Taxation, Depreciation and Amortisation). In practice the figures for Depreciation/Amortisation can be obtained from the Notes to the Accounts, included in formal published accounts. The word 'Earnings' in this context is used in the US as the equivalent to our use of the word 'Profit'. Ratios calculated using EBITDA are similar to those used for Operating Profit in the examples given here. Because of the exclusion of D and A they will, of course, be somewhat higher than those related to Operating Profit. Proponents stress that EBITDA ratios indicate 'Cash Generation' returns by excluding the non-cash expenses of D and A.

A SPECIMEN COMPANY LIMITED

Balance Sheet: as at 31 December 200X

		£000		Abbreviation
Fixed Assets:	Intangible	–		
	Tangible	110		
	Investments (LT)	–	110	FA*
Current Assets:	Stocks	230		
	Debtors	100		
	Investments (ST)	–		
	Cash/bank	80	410	CA*
Less **Current Liabilities**				CL
(Creditors due within 1 year)				
	Trade Creditors	180		
	Tax	30		
	Dividend (prop)	20		
	Overdraft	–		
	Interest due	10	240	
Net Current Assets			170	(CA-CL)
Total Assets less Current Liabilities			280	(TA-CL)
				=LTF**
Less Creditors due after more than				
1 Year and Provisions:				
	Long-term Loan (10%)		100	
Net Assets			180	
Financed by:	Ordinary Shares Issued	100		
	Revenue Reserves	80		
Net Worth			180	NW

* FA+CA =TA (Total Assets)   ** LTF = Long-term Finance

Fig 3.2

ratio groups

The accounting ratios are based on the Profit and Loss Account for the Year ending 31 December 200X (Fig 3.1) and the Balance Sheet as at 31 December 200X (Fig 3.2).

Ratio Group 1	**Overall Profitability**		
$\dfrac{PBT}{NW}$	$\dfrac{90 \times 100}{180}$	= 50.00%	Return on NW (including Dividend and Retained Profit)
$\dfrac{PBT}{TA}$	$\dfrac{90 \times 100}{520}$	= 17.31%	'ROTA' – Return on Total Assets = Return on Total Investment
NW:TA	180:520	= 0.35:1	Proportion of shareholder finance in total. Balance of 0.65 from other sources.
A 'popular' albeit flawed ratio:			
$\dfrac{PBT}{TA-CL}$	$\dfrac{90 \times 100}{280}$	= 32.14%	'ROCE' = Return on Capital Employed, but only includes LT Finance (TA-CL).

ratio group 1 – comments

Return on Net Worth

This is the overall (pre-tax) return that ordinary shareholders receive on their investment, in a combination of dividend and retained profit. It is normally expected to be significantly higher than the return on, for example, a building society savings account, to compensate for the risk inherent in investing in a single company. Shareholders expect an increase in the return over the years, taking booms and recessions into account.

Return on Total Assets (ROTA)

This ratio shows the overall (pre-tax) return on the total finance invested in the business. It should exceed the returns available from a conventional 'no risk' investment, and is expected to show relative improvement over the years. Comparison should be made with industry norms.

Return on Capital Employed (ROCE)

This ratio purports to show the overall (pre-tax) return on the capital employed in the business. This 'Capital Employed', however, excludes the short-term finance (the current liabilities); effectively using just long-term finance. This means that it understates the finance employed. A significant element in the current liabilities for many businesses is the overdraft. There is frequently bank pressure to convert at least some of it into a long-term loan. The year this happens the current liabilities total will fall and the long-term finance total will rise. The Return on Capital Employed will fall as a result, although the performance of the business may not have changed at all! Many analysts do add back any short-term loans and overdrafts to avoid any distortion in trends caused by variations in short-term borrowings, but this does not fully meet the criticism. It is, nonetheless, probably the most popular UK method of assessing performance.

As with ROTA, relative improvement over the years is expected and comparison is made with industry norms.

ratio group 2 – comments

Return on Sales

This is a commonly used ratio. It shows the overall return achieved on sales ('turnover') in the period. It may be influenced by product mix, volumes or price changes, discounts related to quantities or values, and changes in costs. Comparison is made with previous years and industry norms.

Return on Total Operating Assets

Total Operating Assets will often be the same as total assets. But where a business has long-term investments producing an income (dividends or interest), that are **not** included in the operating profit, (i.e. it is brought

Ratio Group 2	**Operational Ratios ('Managers' View')**		
$\dfrac{\text{OpP}}{\text{Sales}}$	$\dfrac{100 \times 100}{530}$	= 18.87%	Return on Sales
$\dfrac{\text{OpP}}{\text{TOpA}}$	$\dfrac{100 \times 100}{520}$	= 19.23%	Return on Total Operating Assets (excludes assets not contributing to Operating Profit, e.g. many LT investments).
Sales:TOpA	530:520 = 1.02:1		Number of times the Total Operating Assets are turned over in the Sales achieved for the period (typically the financial year).
$\dfrac{\text{Debtors}^* \times 365}{\text{Sales}^*}$	$\dfrac{100 \times 365}{530}$	= 69 days	Represents average days taken to pay. Compare to our credit terms.

* Where the Debtors includes VAT, the sales figure must be adjusted to include VAT also.

into the P&L account at a later stage), then the investments producing that income should not be included in the operating asset total.

This is the return generated by the managers of the company using the operating assets for which they are responsible. It is unaffected by the sources of finance supporting those assets. The trend and industry norms again provide bases for comparison.

Turnover of Total Operating Assets in Sales

This ratio is closely related to the 'Circulation of Finance in a Business' diagram (Fig. 2.2) included earlier. The total operating assets are those contributing to the operating profit, but excluding those, such as long-term investments, where the dividends or interest they generate are brought into the profit and loss accounts at a later stage.

By dividing the sales figure by the total operating assets figure, we form an idea of how well we are utilising our resources. Businesses that are capital intensive will tend to have a lower turnover figure from this ratio than those that are people intensive. The importance lies in the improvement in the ratio over the years, as resource management controls reduce the impact of under-utilised resources, or reduce the amount of finance tied-up in, for example, higher stocks or late payments from our debtors, or redundant tangible assets.

Ratio Group 3   **Solvency and Security Ratios**

Quick   QA:CL   180:240   = 0.75:1   Also called Liquid Ratio
                                                    or Acid Test. Indicates
(QA = Quick Assets = Cash and near cash).   ability to pay creditors.

Current   CA:CL   410:240   = 1.71:1   The excess of the CA
                                                    over CL shows that the
                                                    business is not over-
                                                    trading.

Gearing   %F:NW   100:180   = 0.56:1   This shows the
                                       (or 56%)   relationship between
                                                    interest bearing finance
                                                    (%F) and NW.

Interest Cover $\dfrac{OpP}{Interest}$ $\dfrac{100}{10}$ = 10 times   Low cover could lead
                                                    lenders to question our
                                                    ability to pay the
                                                    interest due in the
                                                    future.

Gearing over 50% is regarded as relatively high, and a business may have to raise any future finance needed from share issues rather than loans.

ratio group 3 – comments

Liquid/Quick Ratio (the 'acid test')

Quick assets are cash and other assets quickly convertible to cash. In practice it typically means cash and debtors, but not stocks. Short-term investments are normally taken to be quick assets on the basis that they are easily convertible to cash.

In 'business-to-business' companies, stocks are usually excluded as being too remote from cash (they still have to be converted to saleable products, they still have to go through a credit cycle), but in some quick-turnover retailer situations it could be reasonable to include them.

The ratio is shown as a ratio to one (:1), rather than as a percentage. Historically the ratio was expected to be greater than, or equal to, 1.0:1 (the second figure is always the '1'), but for several decades now typical figures have been around 0.6 or 0.7:1. This has been attributed to the persistent overdraft within the current liabilities of many businesses.

Some analysts now deduct any short-term loans and overdrafts from the current liabilities ('creditors due within one year'), and instead refer to the remainder as the quick liabilities, using the ratio QA:QL (see also the Gearing comments overleaf).

These ratios, QA:CL and QA:QL, indicate the level of ability of a business to meet its due debts on time.

Comparison is usually made with trends and industry norms. Banks and credit controllers will keep note of significant changes in a customer's quick ratio, and may move to protect their interests against any increasing credit risks.

Current Ratio

This ratio compares the current assets to the current liabilities (CA:CL). The current assets are expected to exceed the current liabilities. Historically a ratio of 2:1 was regarded as desirable. This excess of current assets showed that a significant proportion of the working capital was supported by long-term finance, with the balance being supported by short-term finance. The excess showed that the business could continue even if credit facilities were much reduced. As discussed above, the persistence of overdrafts within the current liabilities has meant that a 2:1 ratio is much less likely today, and ratios around 1.6 or 1.7:1 are more common. The excess over '1' continues to demonstrate that a significant proportion of the working capital is supported by long-term finance. Many analysts now exclude short-term loans and overdrafts from the current liabilities for this ratio.

Reference to trends and industry norms provide useful comparisons. When the current ratio is low the business is said to be 'overtrading' and, typically, is in need of more long-term finance.

Directors of companies should be aware of their personal responsibilities for ensuring that the company can meet its liabilities. A reducing current ratio is a warning sign that a critical situation may be approaching.

Gearing

This ratio may be expressed traditionally as a ratio to one (:1), or more recently as a percentage.

Interest bearing finance is normally thought of as long-term debt. Where short-term borrowing is high, however, it may be prudent to calculate this ratio to include it. Many analysts may then **deduct** cash and short-term investments to arrive at a total net borrowing.

In general terms the gearing is said to be high when it is above 0.5:1 (50%), and low when below. Businesses with low gearing will probably find it easier to borrow than those more highly geared. With high gearing the interest payments have a greater effect in reducing the equity earnings so that, in times of recession, the ordinary shareholders may find little or no profit left to support their dividends.

businesses with low gearing find it easier to borrow than those more highly geared

Interest Cover

The prime purpose of this ratio is to show the number of times the profit before interest and tax (PBIT), the operating profit, could pay the interest due. Not all money is borrowed at the same interest rate, and individual borrowings are not always of the same amount, so the total interest to be paid in the period is divided into the PBIT to show how many times it is covered. With a PBIT of £100 and interest to be paid of £10, the cover would therefore be 10 times. The higher the cover the more secure are the lenders (profits could fall substantially before interest payments would be at risk). If the cover dropped to, say, 2 times, then the lenders would feel less secure – and the prospects of dividends for the ordinary shareholders would be low!

Interest cover is sometimes shown as the percentage of PBIT required to pay the interest. In the example used above the 10 times cover would be expressed as 10% of PBIT.

THE EFFECTS OF GEARING £000 Company	Year 1 Alpha	Beta	Year 2 Alpha	Beta
Ordinary Shares and Reserves (Net Worth, NW)	500	900	500	900
Loans at 10% (%F)	500	100	500	100
Total Long Term Finance (LTF)	1,000	1,000	1,000	1,000
GEARING %F:NW	1.0:1	0.11:1	1.0:1	0.11:1
Operating Profit (OpP)	200	200	50	50
Less Interest payments	50	10	50	10
Profit before tax (PBT)	150	190	Nil	40
RETURN ON NET WORTH (PBT/NW)	30%	21%	0.0%	4.4%
INTEREST COVER OpP/interest due	200/50 4.0 ×	200/10 20.0 ×	50/50 Nil ×	50/10 5.0 ×

Fig 3.3

The shareholders in Alpha benefited from their relatively high gearing when the profits were high in Year 1, but suffered from it (the interest still had to be paid) as the profits fell in Year 2. Beta shareholders in contrast did not receive such a good return with their profits in Year 1, but did benefit from the lower interest total charge in Year 2, which did leave some profit from which they could benefit.

business statistics

There are a number of sources that provide statistical information about businesses. Dun and Bradstreet, for example, publish information based on the UK Standard Industrial Classification (SIC). They show tables applicable to each classification, the number of businesses included, and the selected ratios calculated for the upper quartile, median and lower quartile businesses. This means that each ratio gives the range for the middle 50% of the businesses, with the extremes omitted. If the company in which we are interested is within that range, we know that it is not untypical of its industry.

The *Financial Times* provides free copies of the Annual Report and Accounts for those companies in its daily London Share Service listings which are indicated by a shamrock symbol. Telephone, fax and email FT contacts are given at the end of the listing. There is, therefore, an opportunity to calculate ratios for relevant companies and use them for comparison purposes.

A recent survey, however, has found that 5 out of 4 people cannot understand statistics! The numbers can, nonetheless, be useful where what we want to know is reasonably clear, and where the base information is relatively reliable. One problem we see with accounting ratios is that the figures are precise, but we suspect they are not absolutely accurate! We know that many of these values are based on subjective estimates of varying degrees of reliability. How do we value our tangible assets? Our work in progress? Even our debtors? Accountants recognise the problems and try to reduce the unreliability by being consistent in their approaches, and conforming to the mandatory requirements of the Financial Reporting Standards (FRS) of the Accounting Standards Board. This means that the **differences** between one year and the next in a set of figures may be rather more reliable than the two individual figures involved!

As suggested above, accounting ratios for three consecutive years are the usual basis for indicating trends. Changes in ratios from one year to the next provoke pertinent questions, rather than provide the answers to what caused the changes. The answers should emerge when the questions are pursued.

> **changes in ratios** from one year to the next **provoke pertinent questions**, rather than **provide the answers** to what caused the changes

The principal profitability ratios covered earlier are calculated on a pre-tax basis to improve the validity of comparisons, and to avoid variations arising primarily from the tax changes in rates and allowances which occur frequently in the annual budgets of the Chancellor of the Exchequer. Many analysts calculate on both bases.

part

β

session 4

working capital

Working Capital is usually described as current assets less current liabilities (creditors falling due within one year). This is the net current assets sub-total in a balance sheet. There is another school of thought that is convinced that the current assets alone form the working capital of a business. The distinction does not affect the need to manage both the current assets and the current liabilities.

THE WORKING CAPITAL CYCLE/CURRENT ASSETS

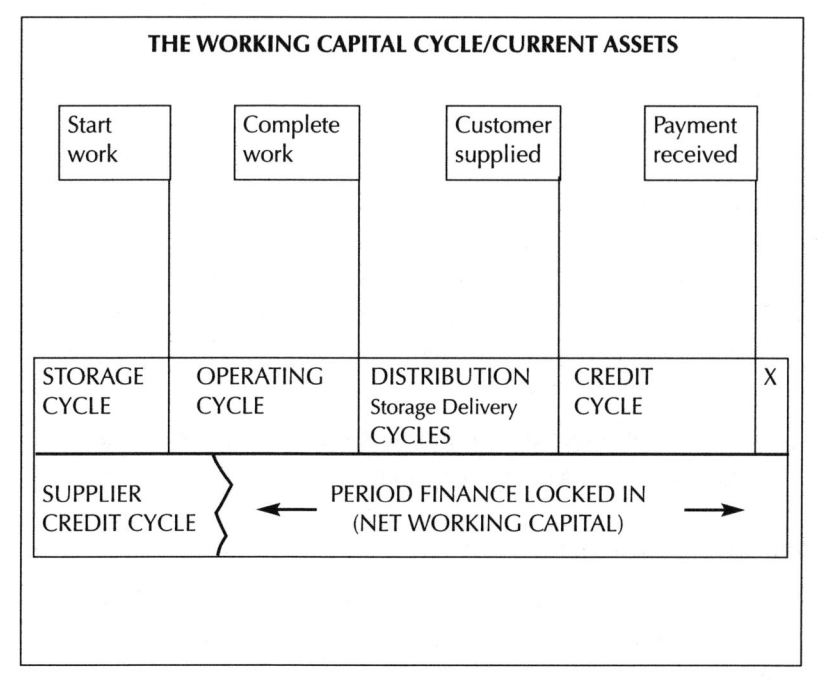

Start work	Complete work	Customer supplied	Payment received
STORAGE CYCLE	OPERATING CYCLE	DISTRIBUTION Storage Delivery CYCLES	CREDIT CYCLE X

SUPPLIER CREDIT CYCLE ← PERIOD FINANCE LOCKED IN (NET WORKING CAPITAL) →

Fig 4.1

A major practical problem here is that there is rarely one manager with full control of working capital. It falls within the responsibility of nearly every one of us to some degree. Yet our working capital needs continuous, daily management, if we are not to suffer liquidity or resource under-utilisation problems. There is an obligation to pay debts as they fall due. There is a need to control the finance tied-up in working capital, so that our return on total assets is optimised. The turnover of total assets in sales is very much indicative of our ability to manage working capital.

> our **working capital** needs **continuous, daily management**, if we are not to suffer **liquidity** or **resource under-utilisation**

cash

The cash position is the most significant of the elements of working capital. A regularly updated **Cash Flow Forecast** (see Fig 4.3) is the main control record. The potential surpluses and deficits revealed show where measures need to be taken.

We should ensure that overall responsibility here really does rest with one senior manager only, and is not diffused over several independent managers. For example, groups with subsidiaries should consider a consolidated account. This avoids the situation where several accounts are in credit at the same time as others are overdrawn.

In larger businesses this role, often described as Corporate Treasurer, may be full time. But in smaller organisations it will frequently be a part-time responsibility, supported by external advisers as necessary. 'Treasury Management' has been defined as:

The efficient **PLANNING, ORGANISATION** and **CONTROL** of **COLLECTION, MOBILISATION, AVAILABILITY** and **USE** of **FUNDS**.

Treasury Management points:

- Control risks for all types of transactions (for example, in the degree of exposure to foreign currencies, or to major customers).
- Avoid, or reduce, lost time in transmission, e.g. negotiate for prompt clearance – this can be particularly relevant where import/export business is involved.

- Exercise proper control of credit (for example, debtors should be regularly assessed and debt/age analyses monitored).
- Review trade credit in terms of days allowed, settlement discounts and monitor customers' levels of adherence. It is vital that your Marketing and Finance Departments act in close liaison in this area. See also 'Credit Management' below.
- Invest and borrow appropriately (for example, short-term investments in the money markets may be more rewarding than a deposit account, if the amounts involved are sufficient). Overnight money markets are available for those with large amounts of cash.
- Communicate dynamically with the bank to ensure awareness of the current range of services available. Banking services are not static: keeping up with the financial services world requires good communications and a wide range of contacts. Some financial services are better provided from non-banking organisations.

Our objective is to ensure that our cash is managed successfully. To this end we prepare cash flow forecasts, designed to show where cash is coming from and where it is going. The timing of these in and out figures is important to our business future and to our Treasurer, whose job includes ensuring that it is available when we require it, and that any significant surpluses are invested, instead of lying idle in petty cash boxes or current accounts. If other currencies are involved, arising from imports or exports perhaps, a second element comes into play. The currency of the contract may not be Sterling. Exchange movements between the contract date and completion of the contract obligations may be substantial. If the movement is favourable then it could lead to a windfall profit. But if it is adverse then an unwelcome loss could be suffered. Doing **nothing** in these cases is speculation, but something prudent can be done. Options to buy or sell the contract currency at the rates when the contract is signed can be purchased to ensure that, whatever the movement in the market, the intended purchase or sales values will be maintained. Doing this 'hedging' incurs charges, but in terms of risk management they are usually acceptable. Smaller businesses are particularly vulnerable to exchange swings and should avoid speculation.

Where a business has international establishments which generate income it is usually better for it to make local payments from this income before transferring money balances back to base – this reduces exchange costs and emphasises local responsibilities.

factoring

One method of improving cash flow is called factoring. A finance company, frequently a subsidiary of a bank, will satisfy itself about the creditworthiness of our customers and then advance a percentage (probably 75–80%) of the invoices on issue. It will collect the total amounts due from our customers and pass the balance over to us, less their charges. Typically these may be between 1–3% of the invoice totals, plus an interest charge on the monies advanced until the customer pays – this should approximate to overdraft rates. The service may be confidential or disclosed to customers, and could include the complete management of our sales ledger. It is reasonable to expect the factor to ensure prompt payments from our customers, to ensure that interest payments on the original advances are kept to the minimum. Responsibility for bad debts may also be accepted by the factor.

The benefits should include:

- Professional debt collection by the factor, improved credit control.
- The money advanced is not classed as borrowing (it will not adversely affect our gearing ratio).
- The certainty of payment is improved.
- It can help expansion by allowing sales to be increased without the need for immediate additional finance.
- It enables us to make prompt payments to our suppliers.
- It can reduce the cost of our credit control function (and the sales ledger operation if required).

Surveys have suggested that the UK collection period is around 50–60 days. The use of factoring can, therefore, have a significant impact on overall cash flow.

CASH FLOW FORECASTING

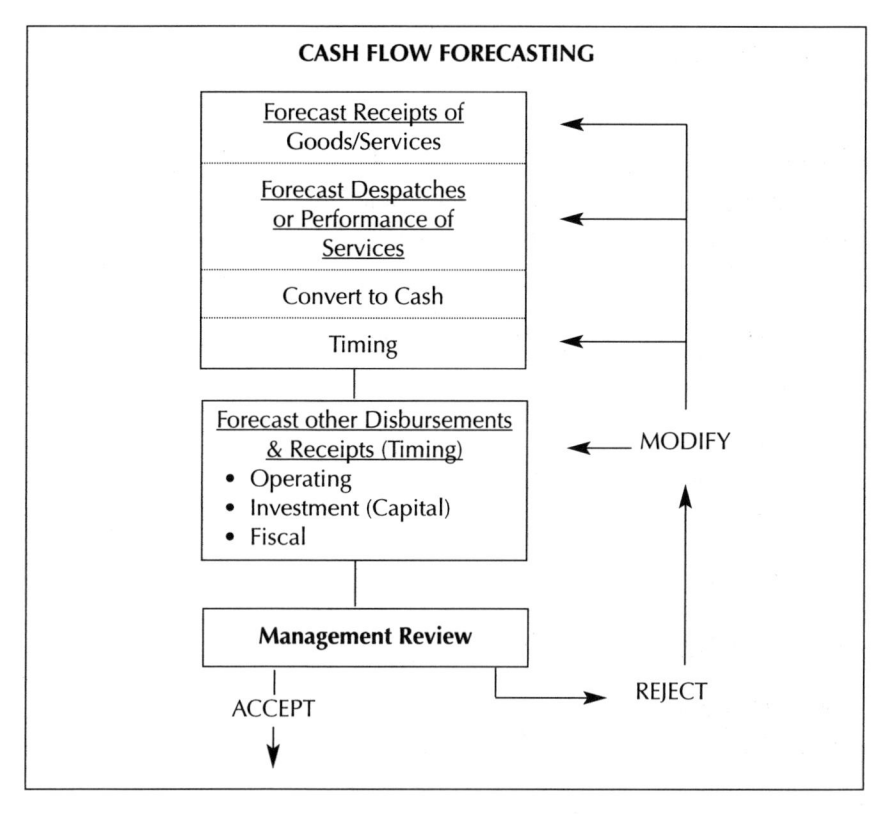

```
Forecast Receipts of Goods/Services
        ↓
Forecast Despatches or Performance of Services
        ↓
Convert to Cash
        ↓
Timing
        ↓
Forecast other Disbursements & Receipts (Timing)
  • Operating
  • Investment (Capital)
  • Fiscal                    ← MODIFY
        ↓
Management Review
    ↓         → REJECT
  ACCEPT
    ↓
```

Fig 4.2

longer-term financial needs

An expanding business will probably need more finance than can be generated from normal operations. Longer-term finance is obtainable from borrowing or share issues. Gearing ratios, before and after the time scales envisaged, and the effect of interest payments on future profitability will influence the ultimate choice. Whichever route is used, it should ensure a continuing satisfactory level of working capital in the years ahead.

MANAGING MONEY

A Cash Flow Forecast – typical layout				
£000				
Month	1	2	3	4
Opening Balance	30	(160)	25	70
Income: Sales	40	240	55	60
Other	–	–	50*	–
Total Available	70	80	130	130
Outgoings:				
Suppliers	190	30	35	40
Payrolls	25	25	25	25
Rates/Insurance	10	–	–	–
Interest, fees	5	–	–	–
Fiscal	–	–	–	–
Capital items	–	–	–	100
Total Outgoings	230	55	60	165
Cash Holdings or (Deficiency)	(160)	25	70	(35)
* Loan arranged				

Fig 4.3

stocks (inventories)

Even in smaller businesses stocks are held at several locations and at several stages of business activity, with responsibility allocated (sometimes by default) to a number of managers. In manufacturing, operations stock control may be aided by forecasting techniques such as exponential smoothing, which can considerably reduce internal demand swings, compared with the swings of external demands from customers. The maintenance of maximum and minimum stock levels (with re-order points based on current lead times) can be delegated to relatively junior staff, or the automatic systems operated by computer packages. 'Stocks not moved' should be routinely reported. The financial implications of stockholding at any level should be known to the senior managers concerned – an arbitrary overall reduction of stock levels to minimise the investment becomes pointless if it leads to operational hold-ups and lost orders! Where work in progress is of a service nature, dependent on human effort, knowledge and time spent, the problem does not go away and some form of booking the time against project budgets becomes necessary for effective resource utilisation. Remember that waiting time between otherwise 'economic' operations adds cost but not value to work in progress.

> an arbitrary overall reduction of stock levels to minimise the investment becomes pointless if it leads to operational hold-ups and lost orders!

Many items of stock are outside formal control systems – stationery, promotional and maintenance materials are some of the most common examples. Consideration should be given to finding effective, economic, methods of reviewing such areas. Keeping the stocks visible often helps!

The essential points are:

- Stock items should be available when required.
- There should be the minimum investment.
- Quality should be maintained in store.
- Pilfering should be prevented.
- Reliable records should be maintained – ideally, capable of replacing formal annual stocktaking.

It helps if 'visibility' is practicable – transparent containers for example, possibly with plimsoll lines acting as re-order prompts. Perpetual inventory, operated selectively, can be more economical and effective than annual stocktaking. Key items can be checked more frequently than basic items to reduce the risks of stock-outs and minimise investment.

The possibility of Just-in-Time (JIT) policies is worth exploring. A compromise often adopted is that of combining the JIT approach with some buffer stocks to cover late deliveries (and often described as the JIC, Just in Case policy!). The objective of these approaches is to avoid both stock-holding investment costs and to minimise handling costs.

debtors

> **The Elements of Credit Management**
>
> We need a **Credit Policy** for our business:
>
> - This involves inter-departmental agreement on what our **Terms** should be, and who may authorise modifications. These terms should then be published both internally and externally. Where appropriate all our documentation should refer to these terms; specifically, **Order Acknowledgments**, **Quotations**, **Invoices** and **Statements**.
> - There is a need for continuing programmes of **Credit Vetting** and **Risk Assessment** by customer, product and market.
> - There is also a need to establish the procedures for dunning (the persistent chasing of debts), the taking of formal legal action and the collection of interest on overdue debts at our specified rates.

The wider essential controls have been covered earlier, but a prime control is exercised once our sales staff grasp the fundamental point that a sale is only made when payment has been received. Taking an order is **not** the same as making a sale! Bad debts and delayed payments play havoc with liquidity and profitability.

The suggestion that discounts should be offered for prompt payment is frequently made, but this may prove to be a major problem if it is not closely managed. It is not unknown, and this may shock you, for some of our customers to take the discount even though they are not paying within the qualifying period! A retrospective discount, perhaps paid annually, would keep control in our hands and thus ensure that we only give the discount when payments have been received in time to earn it.

> *taking an order is **not** the same as making a sale!*

WORKING CAPITAL 53

IMPACT OF INTRODUCING A 2.5% CASH DISCOUNT

(It seemed like a good idea at the time)

Before:	Income		12,000	
	Costs	Fixed	5,000	
		Variable	6,000	
			11,000	
	Trading Profit		1,000	8.3%
After:	Trading Profit		1,000	
	Less Cash Discount		300	
			700	5.8%

Fig 4.4

SALES INCREASE REQUIRED TO RESTORE TO APPROX £1,000 TRADING PROFIT

(Assume no increases in Fixed Costs)

Just Over 5%

Sales	12,600	
Less Fixed	5,000	
Variable	6,300	
	11,300	
Trading Profit	1,300	
Cash Discount	315	
	985	Effective Trading Profit

Note 2.5% Per Month = 34% p.a.

Fig 4.5

MANAGING MONEY

The diagrams show that although 2.5% may not sound very much, it has to be remembered that we calculate the 2.5% on the sales value, but the **effect** is on the profit contribution – a significant reduction of that amount. In the example, a sales increase of over 5% is necessary to restore the profit to the amount obtained before the discount.

ANALYSIS OF SALES LEDGER/OUTSTANDING DEBTORS

Customer details A/c + Inv	Manager Rep Responsible	Total O/S	Within Terms	Overdue – Calendar Days			
				Up to 7	8–15	16–21	Over 21

Fig 4.6

It is informative to have a regular report showing outstanding debtors; a typical layout would be as above. The report could be arranged to show its contents in descending order by value, by age of debts, by responsibility, etc. The important thing is that it makes us act on the information!

Not all debtors are trade debtors; lines of responsibility should be clear for every debtor and effective controls established.

creditors

Suppliers of goods and services also expect their terms of trade to be observed. Within those terms there may be early settlement discounts. Simple calculations (done in the Accounts Department ...) will show whether these are favourable. For example, a 2.5% discount for settlement 30 days earlier than normal is worth over 30% p.a. The **Annualised Percentage Rate** is usually referred to as the **APR**, and this provides the appropriate comparison with bank lending rates.

WORKING CAPITAL

This is, of course, a mirror image of the situation described with debtors.

Not all creditors are trade creditors and conventional credit terms may not apply. Choosing a suitable date for payment may avoid penalties or earn benefits.

controls

In addition to internal record documents, some of the accounting ratios discussed before are particularly relevant to working capital and may well be used by your suppliers and customers (they reciprocate your interest in them in all probability). It is worth seeing how others will be viewing you.

These ratios include:

- Your Current Ratio   CA:CL
- Your Liquid/Quick Ratio   QA:CL
- Your collection period   Debtor days

It may also be worth relating stock values to sales values, or to the cost of sales (often expressed as a percentage).

In each case trends should be examined for evidence of improvement, consistency or deterioration. If the latter, it is possible that credit may become more difficult to negotiate and, consequently, the rate of deterioration may accelerate.

session

5

planning for profit

product life cycle

It is a fact of life today that very few products last for long without changes. Marketing research suggests that products go through several (assumed to be five), cycles of varying lengths before they die, but their profitability does not always match their volumes. The concept is illustrated in the diagram below.

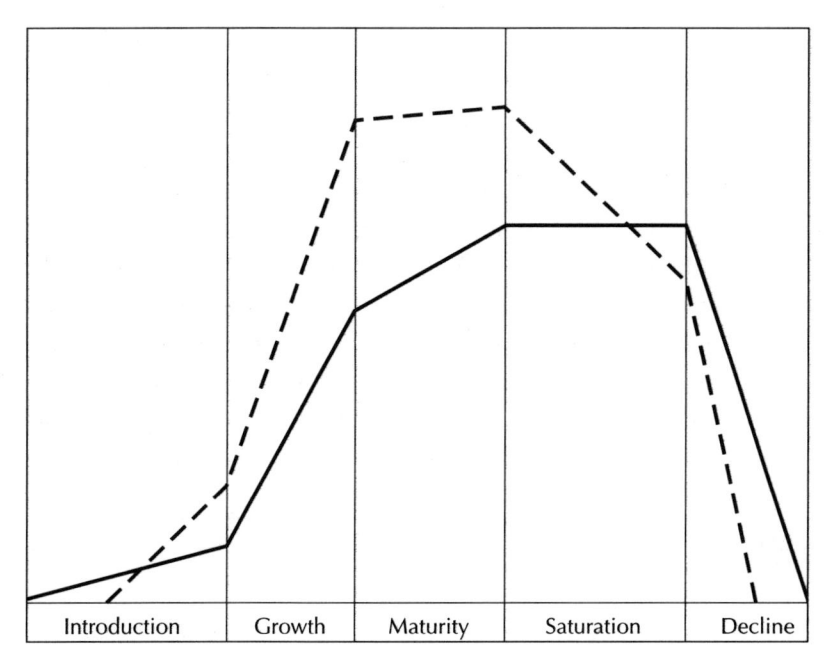

| Introduction | Growth | Maturity | Saturation | Decline |

Fig 5.1

The five stages are shown in Fig 5.1 with the quantities as a solid line and their contributions to profit as a broken line. The stages will be of different lengths for different products and different markets: both volumes and profits will differ between competitors. The concept however is valuable. We can draw a similar diagram for each of our products and identify their stage in the life cycle. Once a product has reached the maturity stage it is vital that we have a replacement product planned to take over. Our new product may be the same basic product with a different gloss, or it may be significantly altered. The car industry continues to provide examples of almost every variant in the life cycle of products saga. The IT industry is moving in the same direction, albeit with a wider product range. All this confirms that we should always be developing products – failure to do so could seriously damage our financial health!

In accounting terms, the manufacturing of consumer goods probably provides the most comprehensive model. It encompasses investment in fixed assets, storage, operations over several processes, secondary storage, physical distribution, credit and cash management. It includes both tangible goods and services, such as training at outlets (for sales and after-sales), and also provides for multi-promotional activities.

Other types of business may not need all the elements included in this model, but their needs are usually covered within it. Emphasis will vary of course; for businesses which provide mainly 'human being skills' (such as professional services) the emphasis will be on the effective use of the human resource, in the knowledge that in many of these businesses you cannot sell yesterday. With an airline the seats available on a flight can't be sold once the flight has departed! This problem is shared by hotels, cinemas, railways, hospitals and hairdressers, to name but a few, who have the problem of matching highly variable demand to relatively inelastic resources – feast and famine rules. This frequently leads to the development of new products, such as the off-peak version of the peak product, special weekend rates, student nights, etc.

profit

Robert N Anthony of Harvard Business School made the point that **'The overall objective of a business is to earn a satisfactory return on the finance invested in it, <u>subject to the need to maintain a continuing sound financial position</u>'**.

PLANNING FOR PROFIT

The underlined final words from the quotation are important. We must not sacrifice the future in seeking additional profit today. The end product of our business is a return on the investment, yes, but not just this year!

> we must not sacrifice the future in seeking additional profit today

Profit provides:

- A criterion for deploying resources (invest where the profit lies).
- A target for managers.
- A measure of operating performance.
- A supply of future finance, directly from retained profits and indirectly from shareholders and lenders, who recognise us as a good investment and will support us:

    - For replacement.
    - For innovation.
    - For growth.

If we accept this approach we should think beyond the present. Our planning must be for the continuing business.

making a start

The financial side of **Profit Planning** is closely associated with **Operational Resources** and **Marketing Action** – it cannot be done effectively in isolation.

The objectives of a business should include achieving a target return on the finance invested, but it must also include market and product achievements, directly linked to operational capacity and performance.

The periods covered by profit planning will be influenced, if not dictated, by the industry, products and markets concerned. Three to five years is a frequent range adopted, but for industries such as oil, a longer time horizon of ten to fifteen years is more appropriate.

gap analysis

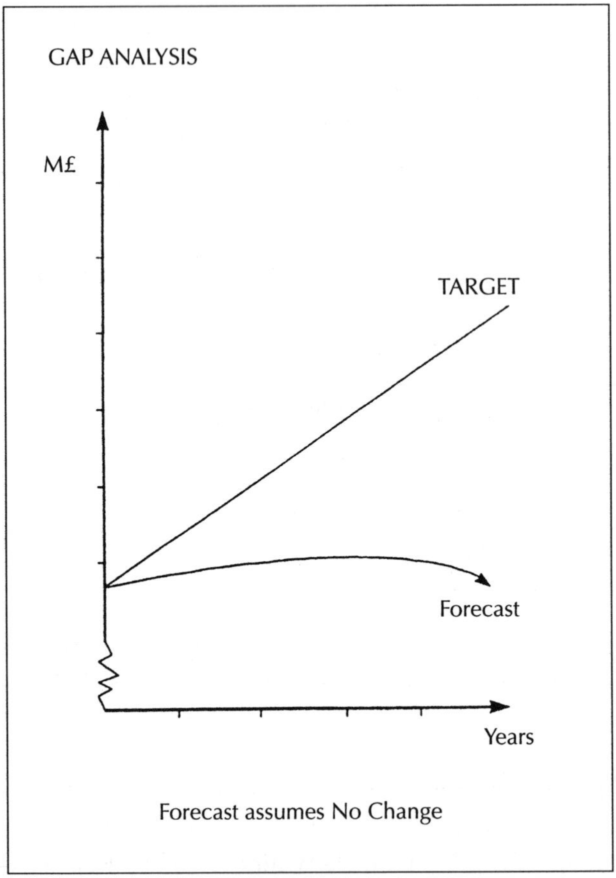
GAP ANALYSIS
M£
TARGET
Forecast
Years
Forecast assumes No Change

Fig 5.2

Gap Analysis is based on four questions:

Where are we now? Carry out a position audit and a **SWOT analysis** (Strengths, Weaknesses, Opportunities and Threats; Strengths and Weaknesses being internal, Opportunities and Threats being external).

Where do we want to be? Identify objectives: markets/products, confirm time scales, adopt return on investment targets.

How do we get there? Strategy and action plans.

How should we monitor our performance? The introduction and use of controls.

product and market strategies

PRODUCT/MARKET STRATEGIES		
	Current Product/Service	**New Product/Service**
Present market	Market penetration **1**	**2** New product development
New market	Market development **3**	**4** Diversification

(Source: Ansoff)

Fig 5.3

There are four areas for examination:

1 We have a current product range and a current market place – typically we know a lot about this area. Can we gain further market share?
2 We may have new products lined up which we expect to be welcome in our current market place. Would spoons be seen as a worthy addition to our knife and fork range, or travel insurance to our household and savings range?
3 We may also have been considering entering new market places with our existing products. Would our suntan lotions sell well in Alaska?
4 We may be considering diversification – different products and markets. What don't we know anything about? Should we try it?

The risks of each of the four areas are in ascending order, and the risk in the fourth is usually very high indeed.

We need to ensure that our forecasting is based on good quality research and, as discussed earlier, it should cover:

- Technological changes.
- Marketing and socio-economic changes.
- Statutory and political changes.

Liaison with the other operational managers and sharing forecasts and experience is also vital – planning to sell 25% more than we can produce will not auger well for success! Indeed, the wise words of that well-known authority, P Storm Petersen, should be remembered at every planning meeting. 'All forecasting is difficult, especially if it concerns the future.'

sales analysis

A good starting point for many businesses is a reliable sales analysis. Who is buying (and why) from us? What business are **they** in? What is happening in the market? Who are our major accounts? Who have we lost? Who have we gained? Needless to say the sales ledger in Accounts holds the basic data – a good accounts coding system makes a range of analyses readily available.

cost behaviour

Just as we need an exhaustive sales analysis as a basis for our forecasts, we also need information about our expenditure. Historically, the First World War gave impetus to this research. Significant Government contracts were often based on a 'cost plus' pricing formula. It was found that not all costs behaved in the same way. Two types of behaviour were found to be particularly prevalent, irrespective of the industry or business. They were given the following names:

> **Fixed Cost** – A cost that tends to be unaffected by variations in volume or activity.
> **Variable Cost** – A cost that tends to vary directly with variations in volume or activity.

Fixed costs (which would perhaps have been better described as Persistent) are time based in the main – rents, salaries, insurance premiums, periodic overhauls, vehicle licences, etc.

Variable costs are found in two management areas. The material content of products is the more obvious and the material content of some internal activities is the other. An example of the latter is the fuel consumed by forklift vehicles in a warehouse. It is related to the activity of positioning incoming and outgoing materials. Similarly the ink and paper used in copying equipment is related to that activity – neither is a sales product, each is an activity.

In addition to the fixed and variable costs discussed above there are **other behaviours** which can usefully be separated for planning and control purposes.

event-triggered costs

There are costs that are contingent on an event happening. Natural disasters provide some examples: fire, flood, hurricanes, subsidence. Because these are relatively widespread and widely known eventualities it has become possible to insure against them (including consequential loss of profits in many cases), so that we may convert the possibility of expense into the fixed cost of regular premiums.

Unfortunately it is not so easy with every eventuality. For example, in a creative business (such as design, or advertising) it is not unknown for several key players suddenly to decide to leave – perhaps to start their own, probably competitive business. The cost of replacing them, and any lost customers, could be very significant, particularly as replacements may prove unsuitable or might take a long time to find and fit in as team members.

Product recalls provide another example. In addition to the actual costs of rectification and return, we also have damage to our reputation to consider – future sales may be lost.

It is in this context of possible event-triggered costs that **Risk Management** comes into its own. Every business should be looking at all its activities, locations, products, channels of distribution, essential skills, business partners, financial transactions, key customers and suppliers, in order to form some idea of its exposure to 'risk', and the related scale of event-triggered costs, including the impact on future business. Our increasingly litigious society means that costs will become higher as time goes by.

If our risk assessments are high then it could well be worth us setting up a fund as a safety net, which we could use to meet the costs of such events, and so mitigate their impact on any one current year. These funds could appear as long-term investments in our balance sheet, but they should of course include a proportion of near-cash investments to be effective.

initial and terminal costs

These are costs directly linked to projects but occurring at or before the beginning and, perhaps less frequently, at the end of a project.

Examples include the development of a sample, prototype or other 'make it possible' expense. In construction companies' work there are often site preparation expenditures (security fencing and equipment; utilities and communication connections; mobile offices) and, on completion there may be dismantling, making good and removal expenses. These costs are direct to the project, but they do not fit happily into the fixed or variable cost categories.

one-offs

These are the consequences of 'management' (or a particular manager!) making a decision intended to deal with one specific situation, but which then becomes a precedent, perhaps exploited by others, giving rise to a whole raft of expenditures in its train. This frequently occurs in the case of benefits to individuals. The class of car at various status levels for example, may have to be rigidly controlled rather than discretionary if the costs are to be contained.

contribution

It is essential that the variable costs are kept pure. They should all be properly identified as variable, particularly those related to products, because they lead to a very important piece of information. Together with the sales income they enable us to calculate the **contribution**, a vital figure in planning and control. At this stage contribution may be treated as the difference between sales income and the variable product costs. From this contribution we have to pay all the fixed and other costs before we move into (operating) profit – a more formal definition follows later.

The following diagram demonstrates the concept of **contribution** and the achievement of **break-even**, showing how price and volume (or activity) levels affect our profitability. Knowing the contribution achievable by each product and the total contribution from all the products facilitates

PLANNING FOR PROFIT

profit planning. The form of the break-even chart shown here is designed to highlight both contribution and the break-even point (there are other charts that show the break-even point but do not show contribution. They are less useful in this context).

THE BREAK-EVEN CHART CONCEPT

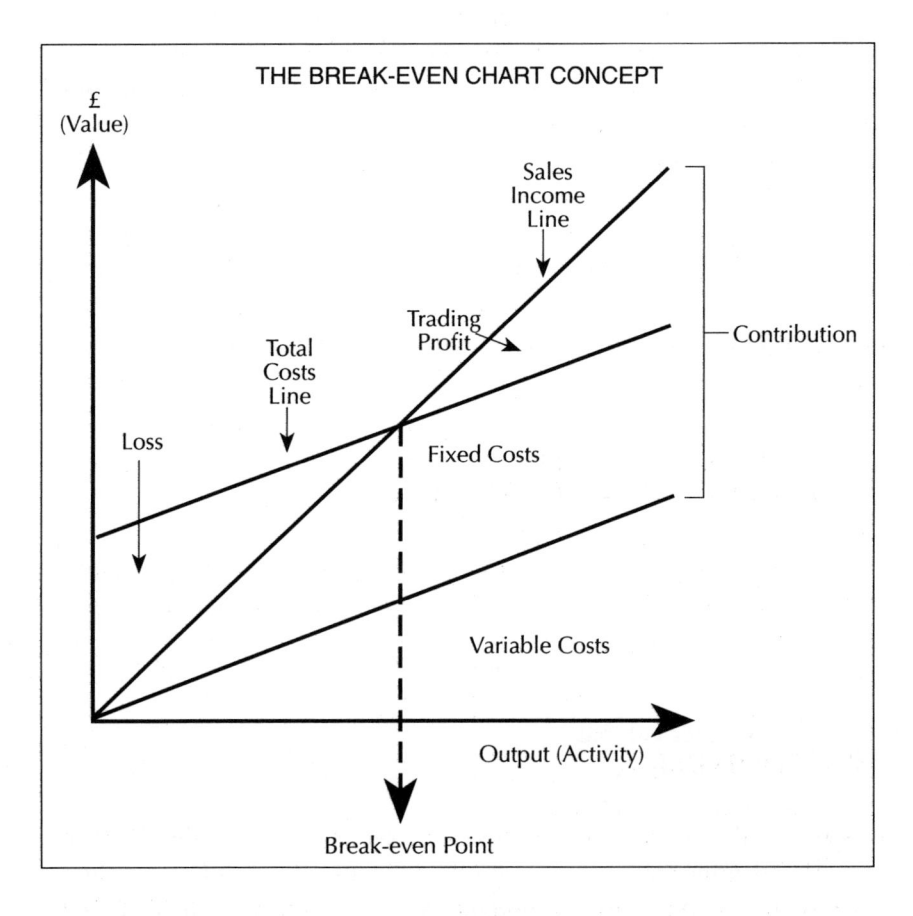

Fig 5.4

comment

The base line (the X axis) shows volume, activity or quantity; the vertical line (the Y axis) shows value. The variable cost line is related to the X axis and rises as the volume of product sales increases. The sales income line also rises with the increasing volumes sold. The difference between these lines is the contribution. The fixed costs are not expected to change during the period covered by the chart, and so are above and parallel to the variable costs. The sum of the two (fixed plus variable) at each volume stage represents the total operating cost at that stage. Where the sales income line crosses this total cost line, break-even is achieved. Before that point the income was not sufficient to pay the total costs and consequently it shows operating losses. Beyond that point we have more sales income than total costs and therefore we are achieving operating profits.

For the purposes of this chart all costs which are not variable product costs are included in the fixed costs.

Where the data relates to a single product the break-even point can be calculated by dividing the **Unit Contribution** into the **Fixed Costs** (i.e. it shows how many unit contributions are needed to equal the fixed costs – the break-even point). This calculation is frequently used in project evaluation.

improving profitability

There are several approaches to improving profitability, some of which can be used immediately, whilst others require some formal investigation and planning. For convenience they can be treated as falling into five categories:

1   **Increase sales volume.**
    Alter selling prices.
    Change the product mix.

2   **Reduce direct costs**
    – Improve usage efficiencies in materials, services, skills, by substitutions.
    – Reclaim waste, change qualities, change methods (technology, elimination, sequence, equipment).

3   **Change the 'make/buy-in' mix.**

4   **Reduce indirect costs (attack the overheads!)**

5   **Reduce the finance employed.**

comment

In general terms, **increasing sales volume** will bring a favourable increase in contribution and operating profits **but** it is necessary to check that the increased volume will not lead to increases in fixed costs – extra representatives, cars, back-up staff, etc. It may still be profitable and, by increasing market share, it may also help to achieve marketing objectives.

Alter sales price covers both increases and decreases. Each approach has its appropriate time. The impact on volume of a price change will, in turn, have an effect on the contribution. An evaluation of the proposals showing the total forecast impact on our operating profits is highly desirable.

Changes in product mix. It is easy to carry on as before but it may not be in our interests to stay with the same menu or proportions of products. An examination of the current range may show significant differences in contributions (per unit, per hour etc.). More emphasis on sales of the higher yielding products may be good for us. It may also be worth checking whether some products lead to higher demands on our fixed cost activities.

Reduce direct costs. Where we have a strong technological element in our products (goods or services), those involved in producing them will typically be looking for improvements as a matter of course, arising from their training. However, an occasional specific improvement programme may transfer their focus from close up to panorama, with very favourable results.

A check on possible disparities between the quality level required of the product and the quality of components will often be a profitable exercise. Developments in alternative materials can provide opportunities to consider substitution or elimination.

Change the make/buy-in mix. We often find we are making things within our business because we can, or because we always have! There may be good strategic reasons to keep a process within our control, or a skill within our business, but we could be doing so from sheer inertia. Suppliers working on a significantly larger scale, or by different methods, may well be able to supply us at less than our in-house direct cost. Again this is worth a regular review, and out-sourcing is much more acceptable today (think of security services, office cleaning, catering, call centres and IT/accounting activities to name but a few – all were likely to be in-house not so long ago!).

Reduce indirect costs. This is often seen as just 'headcount' but this is too narrow an approach. An examination of why activities take place, are they done effectively, could they be improved, may prove rewarding. Remember that all value improvements become additional operating profit.

Reduce the finance employed. The working capital is a fruitful area for reductions – benefits tend to be immediate. Reduce stocks (with care!), improve processing time-scales and delays between processes, and improve credit control and cash management. Any overreaction can usually be rectified within a short period of time. The fixed assets need a more formal examination because changes are less easily reversed.

the impact

If we are able to increase our operating profit and reduce our total finance employed then the profitability ratios rise significantly – there is a multiplier effect.

summary

The planning for profitability approach starts in non-financial areas. We need:

Market research and forecasts.

We make selections
– Geographical areas of operations.
– The products (goods/services) for each market.
– Selling policies: direct, through agencies, through subsidiaries, etc.

Long-term plans
– Selling, Operating.
– Define responsibilities.
– Financing envisaged.

PLANNING FOR PROFIT

Short-term plans	– The year ahead: be realistic!
Evaluate the plans	– The budget. – Accounting ratios: to check on results.
Establish controls	– Identify key factors. – Monitoring arrangements (e.g. Reporting Budget v Actual).

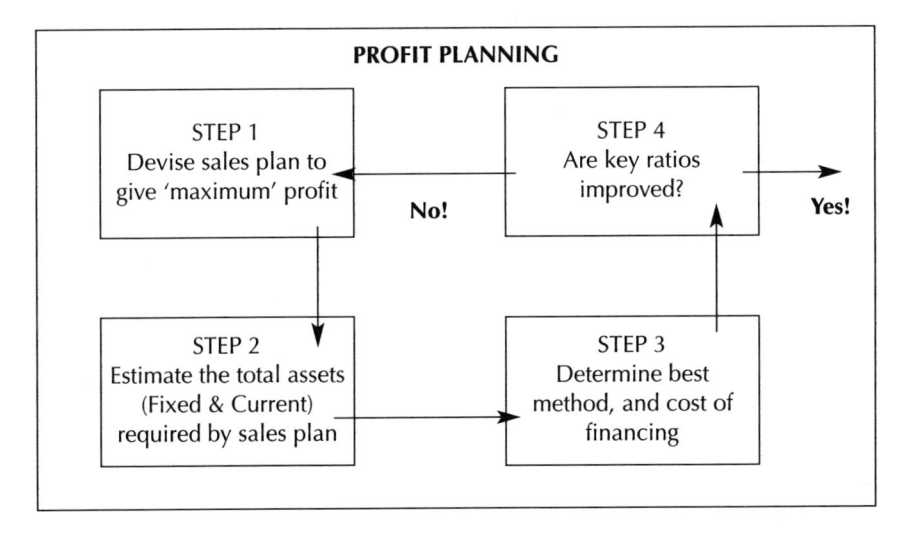

PROFIT PLANNING

- STEP 1: Devise sales plan to give 'maximum' profit
- STEP 2: Estimate the total assets (Fixed & Current) required by sales plan
- STEP 3: Determine best method, and cost of financing
- STEP 4: Are key ratios improved? — No! (back to Step 1) / Yes!

Fig 5.5

Testing the budget by means of the accounting ratios demonstrates the degree of change from current performance, and the potential achievement of the overall objectives, (particularly the return on the total investment in the business). Needless to say, if the ratios indicate an unsatisfactory position then a complete review of the plans may be needed. This cycle is shown in Fig 5.5. Once a satisfactory result has been obtained it is time to move onto the detailed compilation of the full budget covering each manager's spheres of responsibility.

session

6

budgeting and standard costs

It has been suggested that there are three typical methods of control used in business:

- **Current** – we wait for something to happen and react to it.
- **Historic Comparison** – we compare what is happening with the equivalent last year.
- **Budgetary** – we compare what is happening to our plan for that event or item; and react to any differences.

The third one seems to have the edge!

definition

A **budget** is 'A plan quantified in monetary terms, prepared and approved prior to a defined period of time, usually showing planned income to be generated and/or expenditure to be incurred during that period and the capital to be employed to attain a given objective' (CIMA official terminology).

introduction

Our budget is the end product of a series of selections. Ideally it is the financially evaluated plan adopted after exhaustive study of forecasts, capacities, restraints and corporate objectives. In practice it frequently falls somewhat short of the ideal!

Our budget should be feasible and consistent within itself (e.g.

planned sales should not be substantially above operational capacity, after allowance is made for new facilities included in the plans and, if relevant, stock changes). It should demonstrate that the cash flows from both operations and any new finance are adequate throughout the year for the planned activities, and that the returns on the overall finance invested in our business are acceptable in the circumstances we have identified or assumed.

the format

Typically our **Master Budget** should cover four main areas:

- The **Operations** (effectively providing the planned profit and loss account for each period covered).
- The **Capital Expenditure** plan, to ensure that any necessary additional assets required to support the operations have been identified.
- The **Total Assets**, including those in the capital expenditure plan, required to underpin the operations, together with the sources of finance to support those assets (effectively providing the planned balance sheet for the end of each period covered).
- The **Cash Flow** projections, usually on a monthly basis, to demonstrate the feasibility of the plans. This is an interpretation, **in cash and timing**, of the sales, operations, capital investment, interest, proposed dividends and fiscal changes implicit in the other budgets.

The principal budget period is typically one year, but it is frequently accompanied by less detailed budgets covering subsequent years. Three to five year outline budgets are fairly widespread, but in 'long term' industries, such as oil and chemicals, much longer periods may be covered.

the budget and the organisation

Budgets that reflect the organisation and the responsibilities of individual managers tend to work well. In some cases the budget documents may be the **only** coherent organisation chart. Budgets are built on responsibility. Split ('shared') responsibility usually leads to control problems.

The operations budget in particular is a summary of the budgets of several individual managers. The degree of delegation will affect the number of departmental budgets involved. Similarly, the degree of detail in each budget will be a reflection of the data available, or required, and the degree of commitment of the senior managers to this method of control. Broad-brush budgets tend to lack credibility and dilute their value.

Well-constructed budgets, where we can see our own contribution reflected, tend to be good, motivating and team-building. The subsequent monthly reports, showing the **Budget versus the Actual** to highlight **Variances**, provide powerful diagnostic tools that we can use to take investigative, remedial or exploitive action – the money values help us attach priorities to our actions.

> well-constructed budgets, where we can see our own contribution reflected, tend to be good, motivating and team-building

building the budget

To make the budgets meaningful we should base our figures on as reliable a footing as possible. The following points should be considered:

Quantity: Are there quantified elements we can use?

Quality: Is there a quality standard we can define?

Timing/frequency: Do we have to perform to deadlines? Does the work of one department have an impact on others? Are there seasonal aspects to provide for?

What methods or equipment do we intend to use? Do we have any problem with staffing (skills needed, recruitment etc.)?

What levels of efficiency can we assume?

In the light of these non-financial bases we can consider what rates and prices should be applied (and possibly used as standards).

To help in our decision making we have to utilise (but not feel bound by) our past records, the expected economic environment(s), technical calculations and available forecasts from both internal and external sources.

We also have to identify **Key Budget Factors**, such as our own corporate guidelines (if we are in a major organisation), market size, our own operational capacities and people skills. Our budget should be constructed without breaching these key factor limits.

problems

There are some problem areas in budgeting. Split responsibility is one, where either two managers each think they are responsible for something and each puts it in their budget or, worse, where each thinks the other is responsible so neither includes it!

Personal attitudes can be a problem. The budget is sometimes seen as a straitjacket designed to prevent managers doing what they believe should be done. Others see it as a licence to spend, and if it is in the budget they will spend it whether it is needed or not. Both attitudes are unfortunate. They spring from a lack of commitment to the concept and so lose much of the potential benefit of reliable control information. It is not unknown for a manager who has spent all that was allowed under one heading, say travel, to continue to spend on it, no doubt for justifiable reasons, but to charge it to another budget heading which is underspent at that time, say stationery, thus making the figures for the year unreliable under both headings! This could have implications for the following year if undetected.

Where an organisation decides that it would be a good idea to have each department behave as a **Profit Centre** we can see problems ahead. The transfer of output from A to B, based on variable costs, can work. The device of using a **Transfer Price** that is deemed to cover fixed expenses and a profit margin introduces inter-departmental disputes rather than promoting co-operation and harmony.

The use of 'Last Year plus x%' is highly undesirable (it is of course the simplest and least demanding approach), because it dilutes the quality of the budget figures which would be there if the figures were built on firmer forecasts and planned activities.

Budgets should foster **Goal Congruence**, so that what is good for a budget centre should be good for the business as a whole. The measures of success against which managers are judged should be seen in the overall business context. For example, a manager may cut back on a quality aspect of the work (such as inspection) and so show favourable variances. But if this leads to complaints from customers involving refunds it is clearly not good for the business as a whole. Another problematic aspect of goal congruence stems from the introduction of transfer charges when work is passed from one department to another at a price that includes an element of fixed costs and, possibly, an internal 'profit' element for the supplying department. This problem arises particularly when one department or subsidiary supplies its product to another internationally. The question of where profit arises can be important for taxation reasons, but transfer pricing manipulations can easily introduce goal congruence problems between managers.

> the **measures of success against which managers are judged** should be seen in the overall business context

the marginal approach

Budgets should reflect income and expenditure behaviours.

The budget sales income of an organisation should be built up by product, by outlets or significant customers, by prices and by volumes at each price. Where particular customers or outlets have a major share of sales, in total and/or by product, this should always be shown.

A product, whether goods or services, sold at two or more different prices could be treated as two or more different products!

Similarly, costs should be based on variable, fixed or other behaviours. The variable costs depend on the quantities or activities involved in meeting sales and stock change objectives. Fixed costs are primarily related to more general levels of activity and the passage of time. Costs that are contingent on events or decisions are best treated individually. For example, in advertising costs there may be an ongoing basic expenditure that could be classified as fixed but, additionally, there may a one-off campaign contingent dependent on some specific event – the two forms of expenditure could be separated with advantage.

There are two 'control' benefits from this approach. Firstly, the budget can be flexed to match the actual performance, thereby providing more meaningful variances (a worked example is given below). Secondly, contributions can be shown for different levels of performance by different products and departments.

MANAGING MONEY

Three different versions of presentation follow, starting with a simple 'Actuals only' layout, moving to a 'Budget and Actual' layout, and finally to an extended version showing a 'Flexed Budget and Actual' presentation.

Examples showing different forms of presentation

1 The Simple Format

		£000	£000
Sales			454
Costs	– materials	174	
	– power	43	
	– salaries	90	
		307	
	– supervision	14	
	– depreciation	10	
	– maintenance	17	
	– occupancy	10	
		51	
			358
Operating Profit			96

This format does not include any budget information. It gives the **Actual Income and Expenditures**, but this does not enable comparisons with the planned situation to be made.

BUDGETING AND STANDARD COSTS

This format shows the **Budget and the Actual** for both income and expenditures, together with the variances, identified as **Favourable** or **Adverse**.

The variances indicate deviations from the overall plan. They should be interpreted by the managers responsible, so that they can establish the causes and what appropriate action should be taken to exploit or remedy the situation.

2 The Basic Budget Approach

	Budget £000	Actual £000	Variance fav/(adv) £000
Sales	400	454	54
Costs			
materials	160	174	(14)
power	40	43	(3)
salaries	80	90	(10)
	280	307	(27)
supervision	12	14	(2)
depreciation	10	10	–
maintenance	18	17	1
occupancy	10	10	–
	50	51	(1)
	330	358	(28)
Gross Operating Profit	70	96	26

3 The Flexed Budget Approach

Item	std/unit	Budget Original	Budget Flexed	Actual	Variance fav/(adv)
Activity Level		80	88	88	
VARIABLE	£	£000	£000	£000	£000
Sales Income	5.0	400	440	454	14
Variable Expenditure					
materials	2.0	160	176	174	2
power	0.5	40	44	43	1
salaries	1.0	80	88	90	(2)
	3.5	280	308	307	1
Contribution	1.5	120	132	147	15
Fixed Expenditure					
supervision		12	12	14	(2)
depreciation		10	10	10	–
maintenance		18	18	17	1
occupancy		10	10	10	–
		50	50	51	(1)
Total Costs		330	358	358	–
Gross Operating Profit		70	82	96	14
Volume Variance:					12
Gross Variance from Original Budget					26

In this format the planned (budget) data is enhanced by showing what the budget for the variable costs would have been had we known what the actual activity level would be at that time. This is called **'Flexing'** the budget. It makes the variances more relevant to the actual activity and more meaningful to the manager. The **Overall Variance** from the original budget is obtained by using the **Volume Variance** in at the end. Standard costing, which highlights price and volume variances is discussed opposite.

BUDGETING AND STANDARD COSTS

standard costing

Standard costing implies that income and expenditure details are expressed in terms of unit prices or rates described as **Standards**. For example, a product may be sold at different prices according to customer, order size or location. For some budgeting purposes a representative price may be adopted to cover all such sales and be described as a standard. This could be calculated from a weighted average of expected sales at the different prices and related to an anticipated sales mix. A variance may later arise between the actual sales mix achieved and the average used in the budget. The variance would reflect the differences in one or more aspects of the original assumed mix (and further analysis would be needed to identify the components). If the marginal approach were used, as described earlier, a standard price could be assigned to each major category within each product. Variances would then be immediately more relevant.

In standard costing it is usual to separate price and volume (or usage) variances. A manager in the Purchasing Department may be responsible for price but is unlikely to be responsible for usage or volume. A manager in operations may depend on a sales manager for volume!

A major objective of standard costing is to provide meaningful information to each manager, hence the desirability of making the standards themselves as accurate as possible to reflect good performance.

price variance

The formula for calculation is **Price Difference × the Actual Quantity** to which the price difference applied. The evaluated difference would be favourable if it tended to increase the planned profit and adverse if it tended to reduce it. For example, a higher price obtained on sales would lead to a favourable variance, as would a lower price paid for purchased services.

volume or quantity variance

The formula for calculation is **Quantity Difference × the Standard Price** (the standard price may be called the budget price in some businesses).

Again, the evaluated difference would be favourable if it tended to increase the planned profit and adverse if it tended to reduce it. For example, a lower quantity or volume of sales would tend to reduce the planned profit, as would a higher usage of materials in the processing.

Adverse variances are usually shown in brackets: the words favourable and adverse are usually abbreviated to 'Fav' and '(Adv)'.

An Example

Our sales plan is to sell 1,000 items at a standard price of £21.
We actually sold 1,100 items at £20.

This gives an overall **Sales Income Variance** of £1,000 – favourable.

The variance calculations in detail show:

Price:	Price difference × Actual Quantity				
	£1	×	1,100	= (£1,100)	(Adv)
Volume:	Quantity difference × Standard Price				
	100	×	£21	= £2,100	Fav
	Total Variance			= £1,000	Fav

The sum of the price and volume variances equals the overall variance of £1,000. It also explains its make up.

In this example the lower achieved sales price was outweighed by the increased quantity sold. This could influence marketing policies on pricing, particularly if we have spare capacity.

Separating the two variances is particularly useful in situations where two or more managers are involved – perhaps a Purchasing Manager responsible for the price of components and a Process Manager responsible for usage. With standard costing applied it is easier to be aware of individual performances and seek to exploit strengths and eliminate or reduce weaknesses. In this example, of course, we could have a Purchasing Manager buying on price, with insufficient regard for quality. Favourable price variances would appear but in the process area the lower quality could lead to greater usage, giving rise to adverse volume variances. Monitoring should reveal the cause and, no doubt, lead to rectifying the problem!

BUDGETING AND STANDARD COSTS

The standard costing approach justifies its existence where the separation of price and volume variances leads to improved effectiveness. If it is merely providing 'interesting to have' information it may prove to be an unnecessary distraction and expense.

> the **standard costing** approach justifies its existence where the **separation of price and volume variances leads to improved effectiveness**

setting standards

A variety of approaches are available to us when setting standards. It is usually a good start to say 'What are we doing when we are doing it well?' and then 'What is the cost of working to that standard?'

The introduction of quantified targets is also helpful. For example, 95% of our deliveries should be on time; we should meet our output targets 97% of the time; 67% of our professional staff time should be fee-earning and so on. The standards should be achievable given reasonable effort.

the benefits of budgetary control

Effective Budgetary Control:

- Directs attention to problem areas.
- Improves judgments by quantifying (particularly so if standard costing is used).
- Provides an early warning of significant deviations from the plan.
- Facilitates delegation, being responsibility based*.
- Creates a database that aids future planning.

*Effective budgetary control facilitates delegation when individuals within a department are made responsible for one or more of the income and expenditure headings in the departmental budget. An IT manager could decide to delegate responsibility for Print and Stationery to a supervisor, providing an opportunity for development for the supervisor and freeing up their own time to concentrate on other duties.

session 7

the marginal approach – costs for decision making

In planning, budgeting, operations, marketing and investment appraisal the establishment of income and expenditure movements is a pre-requisite of decision making. It is then necessary to consider their nature over the periods covered, and to establish or check the values.

recapitulation

We are now looking at both income and expenditure, but the patterns are those we considered earlier in Session 5, 'Planning for Profit'.

The typical patterns of income and expenditure are:

- Fixed, or persistent.
- Variable.
- Event-triggered.
- Initial and Terminal.
- One-off.

fixed (persistent)

Essentially these are time based and are largely unaffected by the levels of activity over wide ranges of company or departmental activity. Examples include rents (paid or received), lighting, basic salaries, routine maintenance and security, basic insurance premiums.

A formal definition related to fixed expenditure is 'a cost which tends to be unaffected by variations in the volume of output or activity'.

variable

Essentially these are proportionate to an activity or output. For example, the fuel consumed per mile travelled, raw materials used in a product, sales income and commissions.

A formal definition related to variable expenditure is 'a cost which tends to vary directly with variations in the volume of output or activity'.

event-triggered

These tend to be unexpected in either timing or amount. They could arise from an essentially unrelated cause (a major industrial stoppage in one industry, or country, could have knock-on effects elsewhere. The international oil industry tends to cause this type of problem from time to time).

initial and terminal

These are income/expenditures occurring at the commencement and/or end of an activity or project. 'Initial' examples include purchase price/deposit, development and installation costs. 'Terminal' examples include re-sale, scrap, withdrawal and making good.

one-off

These items typically arise from windfall revenues, or management decisions leading to expenditure – originally intended to occur only once. Experience tells us that what was envisaged as a 'one-off' expense frequently turns up under the 'fixed' heading in future years!

basic information

In any form of planning or decision making, whether within a formal management accounting system, a project or a general forecast, it is usually best to attribute money values as the last step. A typical route for any income or expenditure plan could be the establishment of:

- **Quantity:** Are there any quantitative measures for elements of the output or inputs?
- **Quality:** Can we define acceptable quality levels or specifications?
- **Method:** Is a specific method or sequence implied?
- **Equipment:** Do the assumptions include the use of specific plant or equipment?
- **Timing:** Is the case based on performance to specific dates? Does this have implications for values (e.g. overtime payments or recruitment costs if the timings are to be achieved)?

Armed with this information we can proceed with an evaluation using appropriate rates or prices, including quotations from providers where necessary. Any subsequent deviation from our plan should imply a change related to one or more of the factors above, or a change of rate or price.

Such variance analyses can be very educative and lead to corrective or exploitive actions at an early stage. In practice it is desirable for us to concentrate on the more significant items, to avoid the time-consuming dangers inherent in investigating every variance, whatever its value. The Pareto approach ('separate the significant few from the trivial many') should be our Golden Rule.

marginal cost

A definition: Marginal cost is the amount by which aggregate costs are changed if the volume of output or activity is increased or decreased by one unit.

It is, therefore, possible for the marginal cost of one **more** unit to differ from the marginal cost of one **less** unit. This could occur at a point where additional, probably fixed, costs would be involved if one more unit is required – another work shift to be brought in perhaps. For most situations, however, the marginal cost will be the same as the unit variable cost.

contribution

A definition: Contribution is the difference between sales value and the marginal cost of sales.

For most purposes this means that our **Unit Contribution** will be the unit sales price minus the unit variable cost. We have to be alert to the situations where this is not the case – where the marginal cost of a unit differs from the variable unit cost.

a decision making example

The situation: At Jupiter Distributors we have a number of satellite depots served from our central warehouse. We have a planned distribution system using our own 5-tonne vehicles. Our forecasts of depot needs have proved reliable until recently, but now demands are much more erratic and extra night-time deliveries have to be made to satisfy their needs (we don't want to lose business!). Our drivers are currently showing some resistance to the extra night-time trips. We do not wish to extend our fleet at this stage as the erratic demand is thought to be a temporary phenomenon. We have also decided not to seek a solution by making additional 'persuasive' payments to the drivers. We have decided to use marginal costing to help us reach a decision and have ascertained the marginal cost of the additional trips. We also obtained quotations from local hauliers who could carry out the work for us.

Own 5-tonne Vehicles

Marginal cost per trip:	£
Driver costs.	45
Fuel/servicing etc.	27
	72

Haulier quotation

Load/tonnes	£
1	30
2	57
3	**72**
4	84
5	90

The costs for our own vehicles are the same whatever the size of the load (up to 5-tonnes). The hauliers are, however, not restricted to 5-tonne vehicles and are able to mix our loads with others, as well as being able to obtain return loads.

Our decision: For loads up to 3-tonnes we will use the haulier. For loads over 3-tonnes we will use our own vehicles.

Our costs will not increase, indeed they could be somewhat less (occasional loads over 5-tonnes could replace two trips by our own vehicles, and loads under 3-tonnes will certainly cost less). The drivers will be pleased to have their night-time obligations reduced and are expected to be willing to do the occasional remaining trips.

Note that we have only included marginal costs for our vehicles – the other related costs would not change whether a night-time trip is made or not.

more decision making

The relevance of **goal congruence**; what is good for the project should be good for the business – there should be goal congruence!

The situation: At Segmented Composites one of our Project Managers is responsible for an assignment with a client, but finds it necessary to get in additional people so that the contract can be finished on time. A contractor has quoted £64 per hour. We have an in-house service that could also provide people: their internal transfer charge would be £96 per hour. There is no quality problem either way. The project (and the Manager!) will be judged on the financial outcome. The contractor seems to be the obvious choice, but our Project Manager wonders if it would be best for the business.

Our company has, perhaps unfortunately, adopted the concept of profit centres and expects each department to generate 'profits' in its dealings with other departments. Fortunately our two managers feel able to discuss the situation and the in-house charge is analysed to show its make up.

	£/hour
Variable Costs	32
Fixed Costs	40
Internal 'Profit'	24
	96

If we use the contractor, £64 per hour marginal costs will be incurred. If the in-house service is used only £32 per hour marginal costs would be incurred (the variables). The remainder of the £96 is made up of Fixed Costs, which would be incurred in any event, and a 'paper' profit that is unreal.

It is clear that the business would be better off using the in-house service, but, for reasons of goal congruence, the Project Manager should accept a maximum transfer charge of £64 per hour (equal to the contractor's charge), so that the project costs are not exaggerated and a reasonable return is shown on the project.

Solution: The in-house Manager agreed on £64 per hour, accepting that a £32 per hour contribution to the fixed costs of the in-house Department would be very useful in reducing the overall costs in the period. This would be lost to the business as a whole if the local contractor were used.

decision making in the marketing team

Our company, Read Right, produces educational reference books. For our latest project we have identified three possible pricing points, as shown below, and assessed the variable costs for each of them.

	£	£	£
Printing, binding etc.	1.60	1.60	1.60
Distribution	1.73	1.73	1.73
Royalty (10% of Retail price)	0.99	1.19	1.49
Retailer (20% of Retail price)	1.98	2.38	2.98
Total Variable costs	6.30	6.90	7.80
Contribution	**3.60**	**5.00**	**7.10**
Retail Price Options	**9.90**	**11.90**	**14.90**

Initial costs have been assessed as:

	£
Copy-editing etc.	3,000
Illustrations, graphics	7,000
Page setting work	15,000
	25,000

Note: The initial costs are not variable but they are direct to the project. They have the characteristics within the project of fixed costs.

Market research studies suggest that with a promotion costing £5,000 and a retail price of £11.90 additional sales of 1,500 could be achieved. The promotion expenditure would be direct to the project and a 'One-off' decision. The costs are not variable but have the characteristics within the project of fixed costs.

We would like to have a minimum net contribution from the project of £12,500, and are interested in how many books would have to be sold at each of the prices considered.

We would also like to know how much extra contribution from the project can be achieved if we select £11.90 as the retail price, and, if the £5,000 promotional cost is agreed, with additional sales of 1,500 achieved.

our approach

1   We calculated break-even quantities for each of the three retail prices proposed – the initial costs are treated as fixed costs within the project.

Retail Price (£)	9.90	11.90	14.90
Fixed Costs (£)	25,000	25,000	25,000
Unit Contributions (£)	3.60	5.00	7.10
Break-even Quantity	**6,945**	**5,000**	**3,522**

Note that we have calculated the break-even point by dividing the (non-variable) fixed costs by the unit contribution.

2   We then calculated how many copies of the book would have to be sold to achieve the target net Contribution from the project of £12,500.

Target Contribution (£) = fixed expenses (£25,000) plus £12,500.

	37,500	37,500	37,500
Unit Contribution at each price	3.60	5.00	7.10
Number required (to achieve £12,500 Net Contribution)	10,417	7,500	5,282

3   Finally, we calculated that with a unit contribution of £5.00 from the retail price £11.90, the additional net contribution from the sales of the extra 1,500 copies from the promotion would be £2,500. That is £7,500 additional contribution, reduced by the £5,000 'one-off' promotional costs.

Our decision: We adopted the middle price! This means we expect the project to make a net contribution to our business of at least £15,000.

limiting factors

These are often called 'bottlenecks' and they occur in most businesses, often at inconvenient times. Where they are of a very temporary nature pragmatic decisions are probably good enough to resolve them. But where the limiting factor is seen to be a persistent problem, and where several different products are involved, there may be a case for a financial assessment, using the marginal cost approach.

The situation: At the Paradise Laboratories we have three products selling in different sectors, but all going through one particular process, carried out by key professionally qualified staff. We currently have problems in recruiting and training additional people for this process. This means we cannot immediately satisfy the full demand for the three products. We have to decide how we should amend the mix during the shortfall period.

The three products (high-tech chemical tests for foods and drinks) are known internally by acronyms, originally devised for security reasons by a literate obscurant as WINE, LOAF and THOU.

THE MARGINAL APPROACH

We have the following summarised details to help us.

Products		WINE	LOAF	THOU
Forecast Sales*	Units	44,400	75,000	200,000
Sales prices	(£/unit)	1.40	2.20	1.10

Variable Costs				
Materials	(£)	2,100	6,600	19,200
Key staff time – Std. hours		875	2,000	1,920
(Inclusive Std. hourly rate £25/hour)				
Other Variable costs (£)		24,525	79,100	107,200

* incredibly reliable forecasts.

The evaluation shows:

Income from Sales	WINE	LOAF	THOU
As forecast – (£)	62,160	165,000	220,000

Variable Costs (£)			
Materials	2,100	6,600	19,200
Key Staff	21,875	50,000	48,000
Other Variables	24,525	79,100	107,200
Total Variables	48,500	135,700	174,400
Contributions (£)	**13,660**	**29,300**	**45,600**

If we relate these contributions to the limiting factor (hours of the key personnel in this case), we can see which product provides the most profitable use of the limited time available.

We take the contribution and divide it by the key staff hours used on that product.

	WINE	LOAF	THOU
	£13,660	£29,300	£45,600
	875	2,000	1,920
Contribution per hour	**£15.61**	**£14.65**	**£23.75**

Conclusion: The descending ranking order of the three products in the context of the limiting factor (key staff hours) is:

1	THOU	@	£23.75
2	WINE	@	£15.61
3	LOAF	@	£14.65

If the financial ranking were the only consideration we would process the products in that order until we ran out of hours.

The first 1,920 hours used on	THOU
Balance of hours up to 875 on	WINE
Any balance beyond 2,795 hours used on	LOAF

But we also have to consider the marketing view. What would be the attitude of the LOAF, and possibly some of the WINE customers if they could not get their supplies in full? Would we lose both customers and contributions for the future? An evaluated spread of options will help our marketing managers make the 'best' decision, balancing present losses with protection for future gains.

In this specific case the limiting factor has been key staff hours, but in other cases it could be distribution vehicles, machine capacity or material shortages. Relating the contribution to the unit of the limiting factor indicates the most profitable use of that factor. The most desirable indicated financial result may not be the best decision for the longer term, but the financial data helps in deciding what the immediately foregone contributions would be, for comparison then with the assessed future benefits.

comment

Not all decision making depends on financial information, but the identification of potential changes in income, cost behaviours and timing, can often be of great assistance. With an appreciation of these matters 'what-if' assessments become feasible and credible – they may even encourage a broader approach than we might otherwise have taken.

session 8

8

investment appraisal

session 8

Investment appraisal is used to assess the impact on profitability of specific projects. Historically these projects tended to involve an investment in tangible assets, but it is now widely accepted that any project generating changes in cash flow can be evaluated using these techniques.

Typically such projects require a significant amount of finance initially (negative cash flow) in order to generate positive cash flows over future periods. What is significant will depend partly on attitudes but mainly on the size of our organisation. An investment of £1,000 on a computer system may be significant for a small business, but the threshold in a larger company may be £10,000 or more. Similarly, two years ahead may be significant in high-tech industries but five years is a more usual choice.

Our projects may consider questions such as:

- Should we extend capacity or operate more hours with our existing resources ('overtime' or shifts)?
- Should we go in for central distribution, operate a series of depots or outsource it completely?
- Should we offer longer credit to our customers? Would it generate sufficient additional sales volume to compensate for the extra 'investment' in working capital?

We may also be concerned with alternative ways to achieve a particular objective; price reductions or advertising campaigns for example.

Problems arise where we have only a limited amount of finance available. We have to rank the possible projects in terms of profitability to assist in deciding which should go ahead.

operational and marketing appraisals

We have to establish that the project is feasible in operational terms. In a manufacturing business this means that the process will work, that an acceptable product can be made! Liaison between managers will be necessary to ensure that the quantities envisaged are sensible in terms of potential sales, that there is a market of interested customers at the volumes and prices envisaged. We will also need to establish the forms of competition. Will it be direct or indirect for example.

Initial and continuing promotion costs have to be assessed for inclusion in both the original investment and in any subsequent cash flows.

the financial appraisal

Having completed the operational and marketing appraisals it should now be possible to introduce the financial data and timings into the project.

Every aspect of the project that will cause cash to flow in or out of our organisation should be considered, including the impact on working capital in the final year of the project. This is the marginal approach once again; non-cash elements should be excluded, as should income and expenditure elements that would happen independently of the project. If for example storage equipment is to be installed in an existing unoccupied space, it is unlikely that any extra cost will arise in terms of that space – a mythical occupancy charge should not form part of the appraisal! Any preparation costs necessary to make it fit would of course be included in the project.

Taxation affects cash flows. Some equipment will attract capital allowances in the years of use. Corporation tax will be levied on the additional profits generated. The final year of a project may also involve taxation adjustments. Changes in grants, tax rates and allowances are relatively frequent as Chancellors seek to encourage or discourage investments by location or type. In some businesses, in the interests of simplicity, taxation is excluded from appraisals, but it does however have considerable impact on the amounts and timing of cash flows.

the human element

In addition to the **Operational**, **Marketing** and **Financial** appraisals, there has to be a somewhat different study, usually informally. We have to consider the **people** sponsoring the project. What is their track record? Are they optimists or pessimists? Are they in-house or are we buying expertise from elsewhere? What level of confidence do we have in them? Should any modifications be introduced into the appraisals?

the methods available

There are two main methods of investment appraisal in general use, each capable of subdivision. They are usually known as:

- Payback
- Discounted Cash Flow

payback

This method is very widely practised in both our domestic and business lives! We try to establish how many years/months it will take to recover an investment from the cash surpluses (or savings) it will generate. We could compare buying a DVD player with the alternative of renting it. If we bought it and treated the rental charges we are **not** paying as savings, it is possible to satisfy ourselves that, after x years and y months we will have recovered the investment and will then enjoy free viewing. Thus, buying may be seen as a better investment than renting where the payback period is relatively short.

In business a situation could occur where the original investment amount is estimated at £4,000 to cover the opening promotional costs, and £889 to cover increased stocks of packaging etc. (working capital). This is treated as outflow for Year 0 and shown with a minus sign because it is a cash outflow. The net cash inflows in the following three years of the project are shown as positive.

Cash Outflow

	£	
Year 0	−4,000	Promotional costs.
	−889	Net increase in working capital.
	−4,889	Total 'investment'.

Net Cash Flows (positive)

	£
Year 1	+ 1,000
Year 2	+ 3,000
Year 3 (final year)	+ 2,000
Total for 3 years:	**+ 6,000**

evaluation under the payback method

	£	
Outlay (Investment)	−4,889	
Net Benefits		
Year 1	+1,000	
Balance Outstanding	−3,889	
Year 2	+3,000	
Balance Outstanding	−889	
Year 3	+2,000	= approximately £170 a month. The £889 outstanding would therefore be recovered within 5 months.

Payback = 2 years 5 months, i.e. the investment amount of £4,889 has been recovered (paid back) after 2 years and 5 months. In this simple example no account is taken of the full £6,000 of net benefits in the three years of the project, only the time taken to recover the investment amount.

Payback is easy to use and understand. It shows us how quickly we will get our money back within the project. The shorter the period the less the risk involved (and forecasts for short periods may be more reliable than longer term attempts). This is very useful as a first measure of appraisal before proceeding further. Lengthy payback projects are unlikely to be satisfactory. However, the method takes no account of any positive cash flows occurring **after** the payback period and, therefore, does not provide a measure of **profitability** – there is no return on investment figure.

Methods were sought which **would** give an indication of the **Return on Investment** for project appraisal. **Discounted Cash Flow (DCF)** has proved its worth in this context and, in its various forms, is now probably the most common method of formal investment appraisals.

discounted cash flow – DCF

This method of appraisal (DCF) asserts that money has an interest earning potential: it recognises the time value of money. In compounding we are calculating interest on an accumulating amount, which is comprised of the original amount plus any interest earned on it up to that point.

If we start with an initial amount of £200, and it is increased by 10% per annum and compounded, then it becomes £220 by the end of Year 1, then £242 by the end of Year 2 and then £266 by the end of Year 3.

If we turn this compounding approach into one of **discounting**, then we start with a future amount of money and eliminate the inferred interest included in it, thus reducing it to a **Present Value (PV)** at the assumed rate of interest. There is, of course a mathematical formula for this but we can do it rather more easily by taking a very basic approach.

Using the same figures we have just used, we can calculate the relationship between the future values and the equivalent present value (PV) at a 10% interest rate.

Year	Amount	Calculation	Factor	Calculation	P V
1	220	200 divided by 220 =	0.909	220 × 0.909 =	200
2	242	200 divided by 242 =	0.826	242 × 0.826 =	200
3	266	200 divided by 266 =	0.751	266 × 0.751 =	200

In this case we knew the present value (the investment) because we had already done the compounding calculations first (the £220, then £242, then £266). The factors above can be applied to any future amount where we are trying to calculate 10% discounting. There is a present value table showing more 10% factors and those for other rates later in this session.

(a) **Compounding @ 10%**

	PV	Year 1	Year 2	Year 3
Investment £200 (Yr 0)	£200	220	242	266

This shows £200 as an investment increased at 10% pa over 3 years.

(b) **Discounting @ 10%**

Income over 3 Years	200	200	200

Present Values – discounted at 10%

Year 1 (200 × 0.909)	181.8
Year 2 (200 × 0.826)	165.2
Year 3 (200 × 0.751)	150.2

Total Present Value of £200 received annually over 3 years (add up the figures for the 3 years)

497.2

If we had invested £500 in this project, and our expectation was that we would achieve a 10% DCF return, then this project just about met it! In this example, based on a £500 investment, it could be described as having a negative net present value of −£2.8 (the minus sign shows us that it did not reach the 10% target). It was in fact only slightly short of the 10% target. Had the total present value been £510, then it could be described as having a positive net present value of £10. This would show that the return was slightly above the 10% target.

The intervals at which the discount rate is applied affects the present values. The tables here use 'annual rests', that is, the rate is applied once in the year, at the end of the year. Other tables are available which show the rates applied at monthly, quarterly, half yearly and mid-year intervals. In banking and other financial circles daily rates are common.

Abbreviated Table

PRESENT VALUE OF £1 – Annual Rests

Years hence	10%	12%	14%	15%	20%	24%
1	0.909	0.893	0.877	0.870	0.833	0.806
2	0.826	0.797	0.769	0.756	0.694	0.650
3	0.751	0.712	0.675	0.658	0.579	0.524
4	0.683	0.636	0.592	0.572	0.482	0.423
5	0.621	0.567	0.519	0.497	0.402	0.341

Example

If we apply the 10% discount factors to the data we used in the payback example, the position would be:

Year	Cash movement		£
0	Outlay (Investment)		−4,889
	Net Benefits – Cash		
	£	Factor	PV £
1	+ 1,000	0.909	+ 909
2	+ 3,000	0.826	+ 2,478
3	+ 2,000	0.751	+ 1,502
	Present Value at 10% discount factors =		+ 4,889
	LESS Outlay		−4,889
	NET PRESENT VALUE (NPV) =		0

OR we could say that this proposal represents a DCF return of 10% over 3 years.

As suggested earlier, if the NPV had been +100 then the proposal would be showing a better return than the 10% required. Had the NPV been −100 then the proposal would be showing a lesser return than the 10% target rate required, and would normally be rejected.

Where the NPV is zero, or approximately zero, then the discount factor used is described as the **Internal Rate of Return (IRR)**.

When using IRR for project appraisals they are evaluated at a series of discount rates until a net present value (NPV) of approximately zero is achieved: that percentage rate is the IRR, or yield rate. It is essentially a trial and error approach. Manual calculations are tedious and it is usually easier to use Spreadsheet programs which, under Financial Functions, will perform DCF calculations for you.

net present value (NPV)

A **Target Rate of Return** is usually adopted in investment appraisals. This rate will be above the cost of borrowing (there would be little point in borrowing money for a project if it merely matches the cost of borrowing!). It will be influenced by the perceived risk in typical projects and also by the company's current overall rate of profitability. The objective of most projects is to enhance the overall performance, not pull it down!

conclusions

Investment appraisal is frequently seen as a purely financial matter. This is simply not the case. If the marketing and operational data is not well founded then the financial appraisal will be of little value. It is highly unlikely that all forecast data will prove to be completely accurate, but the general level of reliability needs to be high, as the value of the financial appraisal depends upon it. The approval of the project, in turn, is very dependent on the financial evaluation.

There are two financial methods, not mutually exclusive, which you can use. The first, **Payback**, is concerned with how long it will take to recover the investment – the shorter the period the less risk and the greater the likelihood of the project being profitable. The second method uses **Discounted Cash Flow** to calculate the **Net Present Value**, and seeks to demonstrate that the project will achieve at least the required level of profitability. The target rate set should be related to your current performance, so that projects implemented will maintain or enhance it.

if the marketing and operational data is not well founded then the financial appraisal will be of little value

The **Internal Rate of Return** (IRR) approach is sometimes used, or it may be additional to the net present value (NPV) appraisal. In larger organisations generating many projects the need for a standard treatment means that NPV usually rules! Where computer programs are used for the final calculations an IRR result can be a by-product – in manual calculations the trial and error element makes it tedious to apply.

session 9

management accounting

The service described as management accounting seeks to inform managers about accountability in their particular area. It could be described as providing answers to three questions:

1 **'What's the score?'**
   What is the position to date in our area(s) of responsibility? This would typically be shown in list form, giving the budget and the actual, by account heading for the period, with similar details for the year to date (YTD or 'Cumulative').

2 **'Where should we be looking?'**
   If the budget and the actual incomes and expenditures are shown, together with the variances – 'favourable' or 'adverse', then clearly we will focus primarily on the headings showing the greatest variances. We need to look at each of these to help us decide on the significance of the variance. Is it due to a price or volume change? Have external events had an impact – competition changes for example? In the light of the implications what action can we take, in what time scale, to rescue or exploit the situation?

3 **'Are we doing things well?'**
   This is a trickier question than the previous two. Where our budgets are based on firm data (quantity, quality, price, timing, benchmarks, etc.) then any variance can be related to them and judgements made. Where we have no firm reference data we may have to fall back on cruder measures. Are we performing differently from last year for example and, if so, do we know why? Where a mixture of items is grouped into a single expense heading, e.g. 'stationery', it may be worth some analysis from

time to time. For example bulk purchases of some items may be erratic and so distort the totals occasionally.

the purpose

The management information that emerges from management accounting services helps managers:

- Determine the costs of products and processes (not all processes will be directly included in products of course).
- Identify the sources of income (by customer, by product, by market, by area).
- Control costs of any type (control here refers to awareness).
- Plan ahead from an existing position (including short-term planning).
- Choose between alternative routes to an objective.

responsibility

The management accounts may include expense headings that are apportioned or allocated across several departments or budget centres. For many organisations the costs of a Head Office building may be spread across the different occupying departments. This is a useful reminder that the occupation of space generates costs, but control of the total building costs should be the responsibility of a Building Services Manager, rather than individual managers. Some wonderful inter-departmental disputes can arise between, say, managers occupying a ground floor area who object to charges which include lift services which, they argue, their staff do not use, and the managers on the higher floors who realise that their costs will rise if those on the ground floor succeed in reducing theirs!

If allocations of this nature are carried out for policy reasons, it is good practice for the income and expenses items under your control (as manager of the budget centre) to be designated as **Controllable.** Those not under your control should be in a section headed **Non-Controllable** (rather than uncontrollable!).

spreading the unspreadable

At some stage in every manager's life there is a senior manager who insists on knowing 'the total cost' of something – whether it is a service, a contract or, more usually, a product. They will insist on all the overheads being carried through allocation or apportionment to a final resting place. The following case looks at three products. It starts with a marginal costing type statement that shows the contribution made by each of the products. If there is insistence on spreading all the overheads then various schemes from the simple to the complex can be adopted. Two relatively simple methods are shown in the table.

Products £000	FEAT	NEAT	PEAT	Totals
Sales	**170**	**320**	**670**	**1,160**
Materials	90	30	150	270
Staff costs	10	130	100	240
Other Variables	20	40	150	210
Total Direct Costs	120	200	400	720
Contributions	50	120	270	440
Indirect Costs (Overheads)	–	–	–	360
Operating Profit /(Loss)	–	–	–	80

Case A
Indirect Costs (Overheads) spread as proportion to Total Direct Costs (50% rate)

Contributions	50	120	270	440
Indirect Costs	60	100	200	360
Operating Profit/(Loss)	(10)	20	70	80

Case B
Indirect Costs spread as proportion to Staff Costs (150% rate)

Contributions	50	120	270	440
Indirect Costs	15	195	150	360
Operating Profit/(Loss)	35	(75)	120	80

The two examples give quite different results: in the first FEAT shows a loss, in the second FEAT is in profit but NEAT shows a loss. It is not unrealistic to accept that other bases could be found for spreading the indirect costs – one of which could well show that FEAT and NEAT are really in 'profit' but PEAT is in a 'loss' situation.

There are many attempts to be 'accurate' in spreading overhead costs, but inevitably there are a large proportion of them that are so remote from the actual products, that trying to allocate them can only lead to bad decisions and a distorted view of product profitability.

activity based costing (ABC)

Variable costs have been defined as costs 'varying directly with variations in volume or activity'.

ABC best relates to situations where the activity is **not** the saleable product. Administrative and personnel functions include many examples of activities that are essential to the business but not directly related to a product – payroll, purchasing and sales order processing, health and safety monitoring and recording, security, reception, maintenance and cleaning, help-lines and service centres.

A focus on activity costs can be very worthwhile – many are likely to be substantially re-organised as a result. There is also an added appreciation of the work content amongst managers, which can help boost morale.

The phrase **Activity Based Management (ABM)** has been linked to ABC to emphasise that the activity costs derived should be the starting point for improving the value of the activity: in quality, timing or by cost reduction. ABC/ABM can provide a powerful combination – many companies have improved their order placing, goods received operations and other payment procedures as a result of cross-departmental assessments of these activities.

There is an avoidable risk in using ABC that arises when, having identified the variable and direct costs appropriate to the activity, we feel the temptation to start apportioning other fixed and non-variable costs to the activities. Spreading the unspreadable is always likely to prove misleading and bring unsatisfactory decisions in its wake.

spreading the unspreadable is always likely to prove misleading and bring unsatisfactory decisions in its wake

control information

'Control' for our purposes means awareness. The example that follows shows how information can be presented meaningfully, almost as the related events occur. It is based on a situation common to businesses where the product is a service, say consultancy, that is provided on a professional fee basis and related to time. This example uses hours, but in other cases half days or days may be more practical. For simplicity it is assumed that all our consultants charge the same rate, though in practice rates vary considerably with the perceived status of the consultant!

A budget has been prepared and accepted. It shows:

	£000
Budgeted Sales Income:	1,568
Variable Costs	168
CONTRIBUTION	**1,400**
Fixed Costs	1,150
OPERATING PROFIT	**250**

Fee-earning hours forecast   22,400

Average contribution per hour required
to achieve budgeted profit: **£62.50**

The break-even figure for this budget is 18,400 hours (fixed costs divided by the unit contribution: £1,150,000 divided by £62.50 = 18,400 hours). This represents just over 82% of the planned fee-earning hours, a relatively high proportion of sales before any profit is made. It is however characteristic of this type of business, where variable costs tend to be low and fixed costs rather high, somewhat in contrast to those selling tangible goods. However, makers of conventional tangible goods can often sell from stock previously produced, whereas consultants can't sell yesterday, even if they might try!

In bespoke manufacturing and many of the service industries this problem can be persistent. Theatres, trains, hairdressers and decorators (amongst many others) all have their unsold yesterdays, their lost time. It is important that we ensure that we are realistic in our assessments of saleable hours. In the example above, experience tells us that only two thirds of the available hours should be budgeted as fee earning.

FORWARD LOAD AND CONTRIBUTION CONTROL

PERIOD 3

	Hours	Contribution £	Average £/hr	Percentage of Budget Hours
PLAN/BUDGET	2,000	125,000	62.5	100%
ACTUALS				
Assignments Booked (Ref No)				Cumulative (Period)
207c	140	8,820	63.0	7.0%
209a	210	13,335	63.5	
Cum	350	22,155	63.3	17.5%
210	280	17,584	62.8	
Cum	630	39,739	63.1	31.5%
211b	70	4,340	62.0*	
Cum	700	44,079	63.0	35.0%
212b	280	17,556	62.7	
Cum	980	61,635	62.9	49.0%

and so on …

Cumulative to date: (of Annual Budget)

| | 4,880 | 313,575 | 64.3 | 21.8% |

Notes:
*Indicates where Budgeted Contribution per hour has not been achieved

The suffix letters (a,b,c etc) show that the assignment will run over more than one period.

Fig 9.1

The table shows the position during period 3 in terms of the cumulative fee-earning hours we have sold so far, and the related contributions, in total and per hour. The final section shows the year to date, indicating that approximately 22% of the planned sales have been achieved so far.

The manager of each assignment will have more detailed information on each of the assignments, showing for example, the consultants involved and the relevant non-financial aspects.

value added statements

Our objective here is to highlight the value we have added to the materials and services we have purchased (outsourced).

Stage 1 is comparatively easy. We construct an account or statement showing the overall picture.

	£
Sales Income (turnover)	A
Add any other income	+ B
	= C
Less bought-in goods/services	− D
Value Added	**= E**

Stage 2 is an analysis of the Value Added (the E above)

	£
Salaries/wages	F
Taxes	+ G
Interest payable	+ H
Shareholder dividends	+ I
	= J
Re-invested in the business:	
Depreciation	+ K
Retained profits	+ L
Value Added (as above, E = M)	**= M**

We can use this **Value Added Statement** to provide performance ratios and, by frequent monitoring, seek improvements over time. Where we are in a company group we can compare our performance with the other companies in the group. But there is a snag here. If there is inter-group selling, the sales prices adopted may not be the full market price. This means that the value added for each company will be distorted by this deviation from the normal market price. Where there is no inter-group selling or market prices are used, this particular problem does not arise.

Some of the typical value added ratios used to monitor trends and make valid assumptions are as follows:

Value Added divided by number of employees.
Value Added as a percentage of Sales Value.
Value Added as a percentage of Return on Total Assets.
Value Added per Sales Region.

management accounts – classification and coding

Logical classification and coding for accounting information makes life easier for all managers concerned. In large organisations there is a far greater need for clarity than in smaller concerns, where short and direct communication is easier. The classification could include the following:

- A location code – to identify a company, a division or a site within a group.
- A budget or cost centre within the location code – the responsibility of a named manager.
- An income account code – with sub-coding of products and non-product items (e.g. the sale of equipment or vehicles no longer required).
- An expenditure code – again with sub-coding to show firstly whether an item is variable or fixed in the cost centre concerned, and secondly to show whether the item is controllable or non-controllable by the cost centre manager concerned.

Although we tend to assume that coding will be numeric it should not be forgotten that a single numeric symbol space can only show ten different figures, whereas the same space can show 26 different letters. In practice it is often wise to omit the letters I, O and Z, as these can easily be mistaken for numbers!

all good things...

This session completes our course on 'Managing Money'. We have covered those elements of Finance and Accountancy which have a continuing impact on us as managers, and which provide ongoing help for both control and decision making purposes.

the last word?

The last word should be left to Mark Spade. In his book 'How to Run a Bassoon Factory' he opined that:

'To run a business properly you need:

1. An Accountant.
2. Another Accountant.

Two are necessary because accountants never agree and it is desirable to see both sides of everything'.

appendices

appendices

appendix 1
forms of ownership – private sector

When dealing with any business or entity it is desirable that we know its legal status. The comments are not intended as authoritative legal definitions.

The most common forms of business ownership in the UK are:

Sole Trader: Unlimited Liability.

General Partnership: Unlimited liability; partners 'jointly and severally' liable.

Joint stock company: Limited liability – no further liability once shares are fully paid. Minimum of two shareholders in the majority of cases.

Private: 'Limited' (or Ltd.) as last word in name. Cannot advertise freely to raise equity finance.

Public: 'Public Limited Company' (or plc) as last words in name. May be 'listed' (on the Stock Exchange) or unlisted. Can advertise for finance, subject to rules on disclosure.

Other forms of ownership include:

Limited Partnership: Must have at least one 'general partner' with unlimited liability. Limited partner(s) must not take part in management.

Limited Liability Partnership: (LLP) Introduced in 2001 and intended primarily for professional partnerships. A form of incorporation as a legal entity; the partners become the equivalent of directors. The partner's liability is substantially limited to the capital each has invested. The Companies Act requirements for preparation, audit and filing of annual financial statements apply as much to LLPs as to other companies of the same size.

Company Limited by Guarantee: A form of private limited company. No share capital. Any surplus must be applied for the benefit of members and not paid out as dividend. Each member guarantees a specific amount (frequently nominal) in case of corporate financial difficulty.

Unlimited Liability Company: Accounts not made public, shareholders do not have limited liability.

Statutory Company: Formed (incorporated) under own Act of Parliament.

Co-operatives: Purchasers or Producers are most typical; workers co-operatives less usual: membership basis.

State Corporations: Formed under own Act of Parliament – often 'Nationalised Industries' or forms of public service monopoly.

appendix 2
accounting concepts

GOING CONCERN	'The expectation that the business will continue in operation unless stated otherwise.
MATCHING	Payments and receipts are those related to the accounting period (adjustments are made to cater for pre-payments and accruals).
CONSISTENCY	Any changes of accounting policy between two periods must be disclosed and the effect of the changes shown.
MATERIALITY	The pursuit of accuracy is not required if the effect of possible error is trivial and unlikely to affect the overall picture.
PRUDENCE	The accounts should be prepared on a conservative basis. Profits should not be anticipated but potential losses should be.
COST	The historic cost approach is the basis used. Current or replacement costs may be introduced but the historic figures should be traceable.
REALISATION	This is a combination of the **prudence** and **cost** concepts, applied particularly to current assets. The figures should represent a realistic cash value of the assets concerned.

appendix 3
glossary of accounting terms

Within each description the words shown in *italics* are themselves described elsewhere in the Glossary.

Accruals	The amounts related to a current period that may be payable in arrears, or not yet invoiced, but which should be included in the accounts of the period.
Added Value	In practice this is the sales revenue less the purchases of materials and services from third parties.
Amortisation	The annual amount by which the value of a lease is reduced over its lifetime.
Authorised Capital	The amount of share capital which a company has power to issue, as defined in its memorandum of association.
Book Value	The value of the assets in the company's books of account (usually at cost price unless formally re-valued). Net Book Value is book value less *depreciation*.
Called-up Capital	The amount of *Issued Share Capital* which the shareholders have been called upon to pay.
Contingent Liabilities	These are claims against the company which may, or may not emerge at some future date. If material they are mentioned in the notes to the published accounts.

Contribution — The difference between sales value and the marginal cost of sales.

Creditors — (Accounts Payable) These are the suppliers of goods and services to whom payment has not yet been made.

Current Assets — These include the assets held for conversion into cash in the course of business, typically stocks, *Debtors*, temporary investments and *Pre-payments* (payments made in advance) plus any cash and bank balances.

Current Liabilities — These include the amounts owed by the company that fall due for payment within one year, including *Accruals*.

Debentures — These are bonds under the company seal that provide legal evidence of the debt and the related obligations to pay interest. The debenture usually gives a charge on property of the company which may be specific or a floating charge against the assets as a whole.

Debtors — (Accounts Receivable) These are the purchasers who owe money to the company for goods and services provided.

Depreciation — This is intended to reflect the loss in value of assets arising from usage, the passage of time or obsolescence. Several methods of provision for depreciation are in use. Straight-line and reducing balance are the most common in the UK.

Equity — This reflects the right to profits in a going concern and capital in the event of a winding-up, after all other liabilities have been discharged. In effect it means the ordinary shareholders' investment.

Fixed Assets — These are the assets held by a company for the purpose of earning revenue other than by resale; typically land, premises, plant and machinery *(tangible assets)*. Intangible *Assets* and any long-term investments are also included.

GLOSSARY OF ACCOUNTING TERMS

Gearing — This relates to the elements of long-term finance on which fixed interest payments are due, compared with the elements that are rewarded by a return based on profits (typically the ordinary shareholders). High gearing means that a high proportion of the finance is interest earning.

Goodwill — This represents the difference between the total paid for an acquired business and the value of the net assets taken over. Goodwill is an *Intangible Asset*.

Intangible Assets — These are assets purchased that have no physical existence; such as *Goodwill*, pre-formation expenses, purchased 'know-how', trade marks, brand values, etc.

Inventory — This is an alternative term for stock(s), used particularly in the US.

Issued Capital — This is the portion of the *Authorised Capital* issued to shareholders. It may be deemed to be fully *Paid-up* or, if only a proportion of the amounts due have been requested, partly-paid.

Liquid Assets — These include cash and easily realisable assets, such as *Debtors* or short-term investments. The term quick assets is sometimes used.

Loan Capital — This covers those elements of the finance that are rewarded by interest payments: it includes any *Debentures* issued.

Minority Interest — This discloses the extent to which the profits and *Net Worth* of a business are not attributable to the shareholders of the parent or holding company. Typically it arises where subsidiaries are not 100% owned by the parent or holding company.

Net Assets	This generally means total assets less *Current Liabilities*. It is the amount usually described as capital employed, a component figure of the return on capital employed (ROCE) ratio.
Net Worth	This is strictly the sum of the ordinary shareholders' finance, including all reserves. It is sometimes stretched to include preference shareholdings.
Net Working Capital	The difference between *Current Assets* and *Current Liabilities*. If the latter exceeds the former the difference is negative and the company is *Over-trading*.
Over-trading	This occurs when the company has insufficient finance to maintain *Current Assets* at a higher value than *Current Liabilities*. It typically occurs in times of rapid expansion.
Paid-up Capital	The *Issued Share Capital* on which shareholders have no further liability to pay.
Par Value	In terms of shares this means the face, or nominal, value.
Pre-payments	This is a term often found within the *Debtors* heading which refers to the unexpired portion of payments made in advance.
Provisions	Amounts set aside for specific liabilities or requirements of which the company is aware at the time of preparing the accounts. Profits are reduced by the amount of the provisions. Provisions should not be confused with *Reserves*.
Reserves	Reserves are profits retained or arising from non-trading sources and designated for a future possible application (e.g. asset revaluation reserve). Reserves are appropriations of profit and should not be confused with *Provisions*.

GLOSSARY OF ACCOUNTING TERMS

Rights Issue	Existing shareholders may be offered the opportunity to subscribe for additional shares, in proportion to their holdings, by right. Some companies now allow issues other than by rights, subject to regular approval of the shareholders.
Scrip Issue	These issues are sometimes called bonus or capitalisation issues. They are conversions of retained profits or capital reserves into shares, distributed to existing shareholders, without payment, in proportion to shares already held.
Share Premium	The amount paid to a company that exceeds the *Par* (nominal) *Value* of the share is called the share premium, and is a capital reserve of the company. It appears in the accounts within the *Net Worth*.
Tangible Assets	These are long-term assets with a physical existence; such as land, premises, plant, vehicles, equipment, etc. They are included within the *Fixed Asset* heading in the balance sheet.
Total Assets	The sum of the *Fixed Assets* and *Current Assets*. This is a component figure in the return on total assets (ROTA) ratio.
Total Trading (Operating) Assets	This is the value of assets used in the normal operations of the company. It would usually exclude long-term investments.
Under-capitalised	This describes a similar situation to *Over-trading* and implies that more long-term finance is needed.
Working Capital	This is frequently used in the sense of *Net Working Capital*. Strictly it is the *Current Assets*.
Write-off	This is something that is charged as an expense against profits in a particular period. Routine expenditure is automatically written off as it is incurred, but non-routine write-off action may be taken, for example, to reduce the value of surplus stock.

selected accounting terms – showing UK/US equivalents

The alphabetical sequence in the UK and US columns is determined by the terms in capital (upper case) letters.

UK	US
A	**A**
Creditor	ACCOUNT PAYABLE
Debtor	ACCOUNT RECEIVABLE
ARTICLES OF ASSOCIATION	Bye-laws
Memorandum of Association	ARTICLES OF INCORPORATION
B	**B**
Articles of Association	BYE-LAWS
BONUS ISSUE	Stock Dividend
C	**C**
CAPITAL RESERVE	Restricted Surplus
CAPITALISATION ISSUE	Stock Dividend
Share Capital	CAPITAL STOCK
Share Premium Account (Reserve)	CAPITAL SURPLUS (Paid-in Surplus)
Ordinary Shares	COMMON STOCK
CREDITOR	Account Payable
D	**D**
DEBTOR	Account Receivable
E	**E**
Revenue Reserve	EARNED SURPLUS (Retained Earnings)
Profit and Loss Account	EARNINGS STATEMENT (Income Statement)
G	**G**
GEARING	Leverage
GROUP ACCOUNTS	Consolidated Financial Statements
H	**H**
HIRE PURCHASE	Lease and Purchase Option

GLOSSARY OF ACCOUNTING TERMS

I
Profit and Loss Account
Stocks (Materials, Finished Goods etc.)

L
Hire Purchase
Gearing

M
MEMORANDUM OF ASSOCIATION

N
NOMINAL VALUE

O
ORDINARY SHARES

P
Share premium Account (Reserve)
Nominal Value (of shares)
PROFIT & LOSS ACCOUNT
PROFIT & LOSS APPROPRIATION ACCOUNT
PREFERENCE SHARES
PROVISION

R
Capital Reserve
REVENUE RESERVE

S
SCRIP ISSUE (Bonus Issue)
SHARE CAPITAL
SHARE PREMIUM ACCOUNT
Profit & Loss Appropriation Account
STOCKS (Materials, Finished Goods etc.)

I
INCOME/EARNINGS STATEMENT
INVENTORY

L
LEASE & PURCHASE OPTION
LEVERAGE

M
Articles of Incorporation

N
Par Value

O
Common Stock

P
PAID-IN/CAPITAL SURPLUS
PAR VALUE
Income/Earnings Statement
Statement of Retained Earnings

PREFERRED STOCK
Valuation Account

R
RESTRICTED SURPLUS
RETAINED EARNINGS (Earned Surplus)

S
STOCK DIVIDEND
Capital Stock
Paid-in/Capital Surplus
STATEMENT OF RETAINED EARNINGS
Inventory

T
TAKE-OVER BID
TREASURY STOCK =
 Government Stock.

T
TENDER OFFER
TREASURY STOCK = own shares/
 or stock acquired by issuing
 company and available for
 re-issue.

V
Provision

V
VALUATION ACCOUNT

Please note: always check the context when using these approximate equivalents.

appendix 4
an introduction to double entry bookkeeping

This is a brief overview only. Managers outside the Accounts Department rarely need to know the substantial detail required of the practitioners, unless they are involved in system design.

Double Entry bookkeeping could be regarded as the scientific part of the overarching art of accountancy. It is scientific in the sense that it pursues a logical course. It takes as its starting point the assumption that there are two parties, or sides, to every transaction.

For example, if we purchase materials for cash our cash account will be reduced by that amount, because of the payment, and our materials account will be that same amount greater in value because we own the materials.

Although there were two sides to it there was only one transaction.

If, however, we purchase the materials on credit, without immediate payment, then there are two transactions, each with two sides.

1. A supplier parts with the goods at an agreed value. We receive the goods at that value, which is then added to our materials account, and we credit our supplier's account with the amount we owe.
2. We pay for the goods at the end of the agreed period. Our cash account is reduced by the agreed value and we debit our supplier's account.

To keep track of our transactions we use **Ledgers** containing accounts, each with a heading appropriate to its nature. In the examples above we would perhaps use accounts headed:

(a) Joe Soap (our supplier)
(b) Material Stocks
(c) Cash

Accounting records tend to group similar types of transaction together. Purchasing transactions would probably be in the **Purchase Ledger**, containing all our suppliers' accounts. Similarly, our sales transactions would be grouped in the **Sales Ledger**, containing all our customer/client accounts.

Transactions falling outside these two categories may be contained in a **General Ledger**, or further divided – there is often a **Private Ledger** for the more confidential transactions. There are some subsidiary 'books' such as the **Cash Book**, the **Payroll** and the **Petty Cash Book**, which help us analyse and summarise the substantial number of transactions in these areas. Totals from these subsidiary books are 'posted' (entered) in the general ledger periodically.

There are three principal forms of Ledger Account:

1. **Personal** accounts headed by a name (of a person, a company or a government department perhaps).
2. **Real** accounts headed by an asset description covering the fixed and current assets of our business – all related to our balance sheet. The term 'real' is used in the sense of property (real estate for example).
3. **Nominal** accounts – expenditures and incomes related to the profit and loss account (salaries, telecommunications, travel, interest payments, etc.)

The nominal accounts provide the basic information used in the monthly (periodic) management accounts that are circulated to each budget or cost centre manager. Sub-divisions of the nominal account codes indicate the relevant budget or cost centre's income or expenditure. Considerable effort is put into accounts coding systems to ensure that analyses are promptly and effectively available for these management accounts and special reports.

Each account makes provision for the two aspects of transactions. These two aspects are called **Debit** and **Credit**, and typically the ledger page has two columns, one for each aspect. In each case the term is interpreted in the light of the account heading.

The double entry requires that one side of the transaction is the debit entry and the other is the credit entry. The accounts are, therefore, always in balance, as the total debit entries will equal the total credit entries. Traditionally debits are on the left hand side of an account and credits on the right.

We **debit** the account **receiving the value** of goods, services or money.

We **credit** the account **giving, or providing**, the value of goods, services or money.

Debits are	assets	destined for the balance sheet.
	or	
	expenses	destined for the profit and loss account.
Credits are	sources of finance	destined for the balance sheet.
	or	
	sales and misc. income	destined for the profit and loss account.

the trial balance

At the end of an accounting period all the balances on the accounts are listed as debits or credits. Every transaction entered has both aspects at the time of entry, so the total debit balances should equal the total credit balances.

This listing is called the **Trial Balance**. It becomes the working paper for the production of the balance sheet and profit and loss account for the period. Needless to say, if the trial balance does not balance, the discrepancy must be tracked down and any necessary corrections made before the final accounts can be produced. This is a part of the internal audit, but the external auditors will also treat the trial balance as a key document in their operations.

accruals and pre-payments

Accruals – accounting concepts require that we should 'match' income and expenditures for each accounting period. The usual way of dealing with liabilities which have accrued, but for which we have not been invoiced, is to raise a Journal Voucher (or Journal Entry). This voucher represents the amount due as a debit, but it will also include an equal credit that will be offset against the actual invoice charge when we do receive it in the following period. We are anticipating the supplier's invoice in order to get the debit into the correct accounting period.

If a payment is due to us in a specific period but we have not raised a sales invoice, nor received payment, then we can again raise a journal voucher, showing the amount due (a credit), together with the equivalent debit, against which we will offset the payment expected in the next period. Usually this particular type of accrual is not related to routine product sales, which we would have invoiced in our normal way. We may have non-routine entitlements such as rents from tenants or royalties due.

Pre-payments – there are occasions when we have paid invoices referring to a period which does not match our accounting period – insurance premiums or rentals may be at least partly in advance. The pre-paid element is an asset and should be included in our current assets in the balance sheet until it ceases to be a pre-payment.

In the reverse situation, when **we** are paid in advance the pre-payment element should be shown in our current liabilities until we have discharged our obligation.

Deposits in advance of goods or services being received or performed have the same treatment as pre-payments until the obligation is met.

index

There are also glossaries of key terms in the Appendices

ABC (activity based costing) 116
ABM (activity based management) 116
accruals 141–2
acid test 35
activity based costing (ABC) 116
activity based management (ABM) 116
actual income 80–1
annual rests 106–7
Ansoff matrix 63
appreciation 12
APR (annualised percentage rate) 54–5
asset revaluation reserve 12,19
assets 7–12, 17–22, 33–9, 76

balance sheet 17,30
bespoke manufacturing 117
bottlenecks 96–8
break-even 66–7, 95, 117
budget: definition 75
budgeting 75–85

capital expenditure 76
capital reserves 19–20
cash 5, 7, 35
cash flow 46–8, 50, 76, 102
contribution 66–7, 92, 95–6, 97–8, 115
convertible bonds 16
credit (in ledgers) 140–2
credit cycle 7
credit management 47, 52–5
creditors 16, 18, 54–5
current assets 17, 18, 20, 45

current liabilities 16, 17, 18
current ratio 35

debentures 16
debit (in ledgers) 140–2
debtors 52–4
depreciation 9–12
direct costs 69
discounted cash flow 105–7, 108
distribution cycle 7
dividends 15
double entry bookkeeping 139–42
Dun and Bradstreet 38

EBITDA 29
equity 23
event-triggered costs 65, 90
exchange rates 47
expenditure code 120

factoring 48
finance cycles 6
financial appraisal 102
Financial Reporting Standards (FRS) 38
Financial Times 38
'fiscal' creditors 16
fixed assets 9, 17, 18, 20
fixed costs 64, 67–8, 79, 82, 89–90, 94–5, 97
flexed budget 82
FRS (Financial Reporting Standards) 38

INDEX

gap analysis 62
gearing 36
general ledger 140
goal congruence 78, 93

income account code 120
indirect costs 70
initial costs 66, 90
intangible assets 17
interest cover 36–7
internal rate of return (IRR) 107, 108–9
investment 6, 17–18
investment appraisal 101–9
IRR (internal rate of return) 107, 108–9
issue price 19

JIT (just-in-time) 51
journal voucher 142
just-in-time (JIT) 51

key budget factors 78

ledgers 139–141
lenders 16
length of chain 8
limiting factors 96–8
liquid ratio 35
loans 16
location code 120
longer-term finance 49

management accounting 113–121
marginal costs 91, 92–4
market price 16
market research 70–71
marketing appraisal 102

negative cash flow 101
net current assets 17
net present value (NPV) 107–8
NI contributions 16
nominal accounts 140
NPV (net present value) 107–8

one-off costs 66, 90

operating profit 29, 68
operational appraisal 102
operations 76
overall variance 82

PAYE (pay as you earn) 16
PBIT (profit before income and tax) 37
PESTLE 19
preference shares 18–19
pre-payment 16–17, 142
price variance 83
pricing 69
product and market strategies 63
product life cycle 59–60
product mix 69
profit and loss statement 29, 115
profitability 59–71

quantity variance 82, 83–4
quick assets 35

ratios 27–39, 71
real accounts 140
recapitulation 89–90
recovering finance 9
'reducing balance' depreciation 10
reservoir 20
retained profits 15, 22
return on capital employed (ROCE) 31–2
return on investment (ROI) 105
return on net worth 31
return on sales 32
return on total assets (ROTA) 31–2
return on total operating assets 32
revaluation 12
revenue reserves 15, 22
rights issues 19
risk management 65
ROCE (return on capital employed) 31–2
ROI (return on investment) 105
ROTA (return on total assets) 31–2

sales ledger 140

INDEX

sales volume 69
scale of operation 8
seasonality 8
share premium 19–20
SIC (standard industrial classification) 38
solvency and security ratios 34–8
speed of sale 8
standard costing 83
standard industrial classification (SIC) 38
statistics 38
stock control 50–51, 70
Stock Exchange 16
'straight line' depreciation 10, 12
'sum of the digits' depreciation 11
SWOT analysis 62

tangible assets 9–12, 16, 19
target rate of return 108
taxation 102

terminal costs 66, 90
total assets 7, 76
total cost 115–6
trade creditors 16
transfer price 78–9
treasury management 46–7
trial balance 141
turnover of total operating assets in sales 33

underwriting 19
unit contribution 68, 92

value added statements 119
variable costs 64, 67–8, 79, 82, 90, 94–5, 97, 116
variances 78–9, 81–5, 91
VAT 16
volume variance 82, 83–4

working capital 45–55

NOTES

NOTES

NOTES

NOTES

Also available from CIM Publishing

managing change
regenerating business
by Marie McHugh

Marie McHugh's book shows you how to acquire and develop skills to enable you to become a better and more effective manager of change. It examines a range of issues associated with the process of managing change in organisations, and with practical tasks and exercises, the book equips you with the knowledge and ability to ensure change is implemented smoothly and successfully.

Marie McHugh is Reader in Organisational Behaviour at the University of Ulster. ISBN 0 902130 61 7

managing time
loving every minute
by Peter Green

Time management is one of the most valuable business skills a professional can have; CIM Course Director Peter Green shows how to find time for the important as well as the urgent, how to say no without being unprofessional, and how to cope with changed priorities, interruptions and hectic schedules. This book will help you achieve a greater amount of work in less time, stay calm and focused and enjoy your working routine.

Peter Green is a sales and management development consultant and runs CIM's time management course. ISBN 0 902130 59 5

managing stress
second edition
by Derek Roger

available March 2002

Fully revised and updated, Derek Roger's seminal text on stress management in the workplace offers invaluable advice on how to stop a difficult situation becoming an unbearable one. Coping strategies show you how to deal with stress calmly, methodically and practically. The distillation of extensive research, the book shows how many methods of stress management commonly employed can actually be counter-productive, and in a series of practical sessions shows how to manage difficult issues without incurring stress.

Derek Roger is a Senior Lecturer in Psychology and Director of the Stress Research Unit at the University of York. ISBN 0 902130 60 9

All these books are available from CIM Publishing for £9.99 each, including p&p. To order, telephone CIM Direct on 01628 427427, email cimdirect@cim.co.uk or visit www.cim.co.uk.